DISCARD

COUNTRY TOPICS FOR CRAFT PROJECTS

FRANCE

Anita Ganeri and Rachel Wright

Illustrated by John Shackell

FRANKLIN WATTS

NEW YORK • CHICAGO • LONDON • TORONTO • SYDNEY

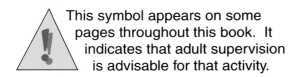
This symbol appears on some pages throughout this book. It indicates that adult supervision is advisable for that activity.

Franklin Watts
95 Madison Avenue
New York, N. Y. 10016

10 9 8 7 6 5 4 3 2 1

Library of Congress Cataloging-in-Publication Data

Ganeri, Anita
    France / by Anita Ganeri and Rachel Wright.
        p. cm. — (Country topics)
    Includes index.
    Summary: Introduces the geographical, historical, and social aspects of everyday life in France, examining the different regions, trade, agriculture, and school and homelife. Includes modelmaking, recipes, games, and other activities.
    ISBN 0-531-14256-6
    1. France–Social life and customs–20th century–Juvenile literature.
[1. France.] I. Wright, Rachel. II. Title. III. Series.
DC33,7.B597   1993
944.083–dc20   92-27136
                                                       CIP AC

Editor: Hazel Poole
Designer: Sally Boothroyd
Photography: Peter Millard
Artwork: John Shackell and Teri Gower
Picture research: Ambreen Husain, Annabel Martin, Juliet Duff

Printed in the United Kingdom

CONTENTS

Introducing France

BIENVENUE A LA FRANCE!

Welcome to France! Before you start to explore, here are a few useful facts about the country.

FRANCE IN THE WORLD

France is the biggest country in Western Europe, covering an area of about 224,037 square miles (544,000 sq km), including the island of Corsica. Its capital is Paris, one of the world's most famous and most glamorous cities. As you can see from the map, France has a long coastline with the Atlantic Ocean and Mediterranean Sea. On land, it has borders with Spain, Italy, Switzerland, Germany, Luxembourg, and Belgium. It is separated from Great Britain by the English Channel.

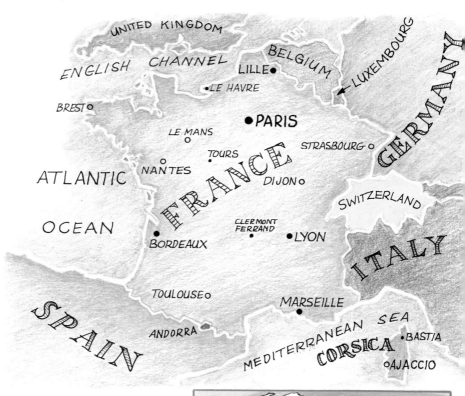

FLYING THE FLAG

The French flag is called *le tricolore* (the tricolor) because it has three stripes of blue, red, and white. The colors have special meanings. Red and blue are the colors of Paris and white was once the color of French royalty. The present flag was first used in the French Revolution of 1789.

France is a republic – its official title is *République Française.* The president is the head of state and is elected for seven years at a time. The prime minister leads the government. Parliament is made up of the National Assembly and the Senate.

FRENCH MONEY AND STAMPS

The French currency is called the *franc*, written as F or f. One franc is divided into 100 *centimes* (c). You can get bank notes for the following amounts—20, 50, 100, 200 and 500 francs. There are coins for 10, 5, 2, 1 and $^1/_2$ francs, as well as for 20, 10 and 5 centimes.

Even French stamps haven't escaped from the influence of the French Revolution. They show the figure of a woman, known as Marianne —another emblem of the Revolution.

On one side of French coins are the words, *Liberté, Egalité, Fraternité*–Liberty, Equality, Fraternity–the motto of the French Revolution.

LA MARSEILLAISE

The French national anthem is called *La Marseillaise*. It was composed by a solider, Claude-Joseph Rouget De Lisle, as a rousing marching song for the revolutionary army as they walked from Marseille to Paris in 1792. It became the national song in 1795, and the national anthem in 1879.

KEEP TO THE RIGHT

In France, you drive on the right-hand side of the street so cars have their steering wheels on the left. You can tell which part of France a car comes from by its license plate. Different *départements* (regions) have their own numbers, which they use on cars and as postal codes.

Say it in French
le drapeau - flag
le timbre - stamp
l'argent - money
la France - France
les Français - the French
la carte - map

5

Around France

There are many different parts of France to visit–rolling countryside, snow-capped mountains, tree-lined rivers, and sandy beaches. There are also many ancient buildings and historic landmarks to see.

Average temperatures		
Place	**January**	**July**
Paris	32° F	75° F
Nice	48° F	80° F
Bordeaux	45° F	78° F

WHAT DIALECT?

Several different languages and dialects are spoken in France. It all depends on the area. For example, in parts of Brittany, some people speak a language known as Breton, and in the area around the border with Spain you can hear Basque being spoken. Also, in the Alsace and Lorraine regions, a German dialect can be heard.

MONT-ST-MICHEL

Mont-St-Michel is a small island off the coast of Normandy. At high tide, the island is surrounded by water. At low tide, however, you can drive or walk to it across the seabed. Millions of people a year visit the picturesque abbey and town on the island.

FRENCH GEOGRAPHY

The landscape of France changes from place to place. This map shows the main geographical regions and the main mountains and rivers. It also shows a few famous places you might like to visit.

Like the scenery, the weather also varies from place to place. The north of France has warm summers and cold winters. The south has very hot summers and mild winters. It is also wetter in the north. Mountainous areas in the east and south have heavy snow in winter.

July and August are the hottest months of the year. The south is sometimes hit by a fierce, cold wind called the *mistral* which can destroy farmers' crops.

EIFFEL TOWER

The Eiffel Tower is one of Paris's most famous landmarks. It was built for the Paris *Exposition* (exhibition) of 1889 and contains 9,700 tons of iron. It is 1,000 feet (300.5 m) high. It's a steep climb to the top but you get a good view of the city.

THE FRENCH RIVIERA

The sunny south coast is famous for its resorts, such as Nice and Cannes. These attract tourists from all over the world–often very wealthy ones! This stretch of coastline is known as the Riviera or the Côte d'Azur–the sky-blue coast.

MONT BLANC

Mont Blanc is the highest mountain in the Alps, at 15,781 feet (4,810 m). The nearby town of Chamonix is popular with mountaineers and skiers. The first winter Olympics were held in Chamonix in 1924. Other famous ski resorts include Val d'Isère and Courchevel.

CHATEAU DE CHAMBORD

The River Loire is famous for its beautiful stately homes, or châteaux. The château of Chambord was built by King François I in 1519. It is a mass of turrets, chimneys, and bell towers. It has more than 15 staircases. One is a double spiral—two people can walk up or down it without ever meeting!

Say it in French

l'été - summer   la pluie - rain
l'hiver - winter   la plage - beach
le temps - weather   la montagne - mountain
le soleil - sun   la tour Eiffel - Eiffel tower
le château - castle, stately home

Food and Drink

French restaurants, food, and drink are famous all over the world. In France itself, food is taken very seriously indeed.

SHOPPING FOR FOOD

French people love food and take a lot of trouble over what they eat. They are careful about what they buy, spending time and money on finding the freshest, tastiest ingredients. Most people go to the supermarket once a week, but they also visit small, specialty shops and the local market. Every French town has its market day, when farmers sell their fresh fruit, vegetables, eggs and cheese. There are street markets in big cities, such as Paris, too.

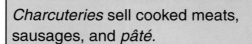

Shopping list
le pain — bread
le lait — milk
le fromage — cheese
les oeufs — eggs
le sucre — sugar
les légumes — vegetables
le poisson — fish
le café — coffee
le vin — wine
le chocolat — chocolate

France is also famous for its wine, champagne, and brandy. There are several important wine-growing areas, such as the Loire valley, where you can see vineyards for miles around.

Boulangeries sell all kinds of bread. The long French stick, called a *baguette*, is crisp outside and chewy inside.

Patisseries sell wonderful cakes and pastries. Try a fruit *tarte* or a cream-filled *éclair*.

Charcuteries sell cooked meats, sausages, and *pâté*.

Fromageries are special shops selling cheese. There are over 300 kinds of French cheese, made from cow's, sheep's, and goat's milk.

FRENCH COOKING

French chefs are famous for their cooking skills. The food varies a little in each part of France because chefs make use of the different local ingredients. In the north, where cows graze on the lush grass, lots of butter and cream are used. Brittany is famous for

its *crêpes*. Along the coasts seafood is very popular, with dishes such as *bouillabaisse* (fish soup) and *moules* (mussels). Further south, food is flavored with local herbs, garlic, and olive oil.

As well as cooking at home, French people enjoy eating out in cafés and restaurants. The whole family may go to a restaurant for lunch at the weekend. The meal will consist of three or four courses–for example soup, meat or fish with vegetables, cheese, and fruit or a dessert to finish.

People take their time over their food–lunch may last the whole afternoon!

CROISSANT MAZE

You have been kidnapped by food fanatics and locked up in the sugar room of a croissant factory. To make your escape, you can only enter those rooms which are named after a food or drink. You have 60 seconds to make your getaway... starting now!

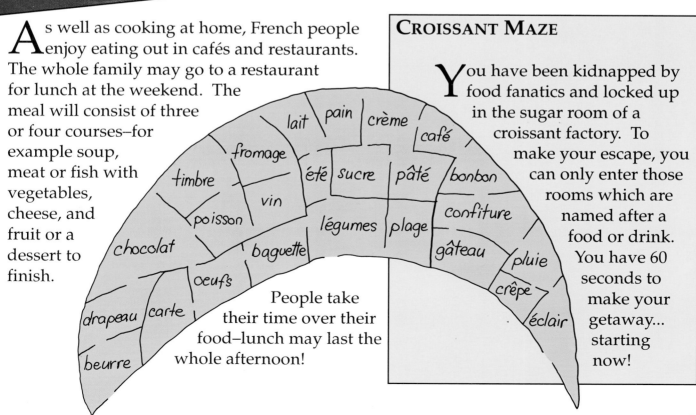

lait · pain · crème · café · fromage · été · sucre · pâté · bonbon · timbre · vin · confiture · poisson · légumes · plage · chocolat · baguette · gâteau · pluie · oeufs · crêpe · drapeau · carte · éclair · beurre

A Taste of France

French cafés are famous for their terraces, where customers can relax with a drink or a snack and watch the world go by. Most cafés display a list of snacks in their window. These usually include pizza, omelettes, baguette sandwiches, and *croque-monsieur*.

Croque-monsieur is easy to make and delicious to eat, as you'll discover if you try the recipe below.

YOU WILL NEED:

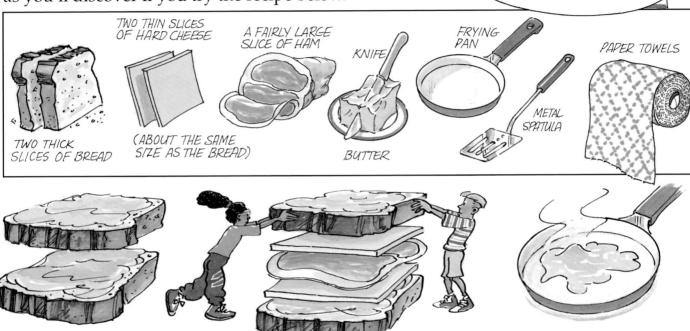

TWO THIN SLICES OF HARD CHEESE

A FAIRLY LARGE SLICE OF HAM

KNIFE

FRYING PAN

PAPER TOWELS

METAL SPATULA

TWO THICK SLICES OF BREAD

(ABOUT THE SAME SIZE AS THE BREAD)

BUTTER

1. Butter both slices of bread on both sides.

2. Cover one of the pieces of bread with a slice of cheese. Then add the ham, the other slice of cheese, and the second slice of bread —to make a double-decker sandwich.

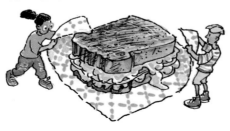

3. Melt a small lump of butter in the frying pan over a low heat.

4. Fry the sandwich for three to five minutes on each side until the bread is golden brown and the cheese is beginning to melt.

5. When your sandwich is ready, carefully lift it out of the pan with the metal spatula, drain it on some paper towels and dig in!

Croque monsieur means "Mr. Crunch!"

Cafés in France sell a wide range of hot and cold drinks, including *citron pressé*, or freshly squeezed lemonade

To make your own *citron pressé*...

YOU WILL NEED:

MINERAL WATER

SOME TALL GLASSES

ICE

SUPERFINE SUGAR

LEMONS (ONE FOR EACH GLASS)

LEMON SQUEEZER

KNIFE

HAMMER

TABLESPOON

CLEAN DISH TOWEL

1. Cut the lemons in half and squeeze the juice into the glasses.

2. Add a tablespoon of sugar to each glass.

3. Wrap the ice in the dish towel and tap it carefully with the hammer until it is crushed.

4. Add the crushed ice to the sugar and juice. Fill each glass with water and serve at once.

Prices in cafés vary, depending on whether you sit at a table inside, stand at the bar, or sit outside on the terrace.

Life in France

WHERE PEOPLE LIVE

Almost three-quarters of French people live in towns and cities. Many live in apartments–either in old buildings in the center of town or in modern housing complexes on the outskirts. In many French cities there are laws forbidding the building of high-rise buildings in the city center. People often live in the suburbs and commute into the city every day to work.

About one-quarter of French people live in the countryside, many in small villages. These usually have a village square, with a church and some small stores. Houses are often small and traditional with shutters at the windows. Some people live in farmhouses.

WHAT PEOPLE DO

Many people in the big cities work in factories making cars, electronic goods, and aircraft. In the countryside, some people are farmers. They raise sheep and cows, and grow crops such as wheat, apples, grapes, and sugar beet. In Paris, the Alps and along the Côte d'Azur, many people are employed in the tourist industry.

POLICE

In France, there are two kinds of police. *Les gendarmes* work in the country, and *les agents de police* work in the town. The emergency telephone number for the police is 17.

Say it in French
le fermier - farmer
le professeur - teacher
le médecin - doctor
l'ouvrier - factory worker
le chef - chef
le facteur - postman

GOING TO SCHOOL

French children must go to school from the ages of 6 - 16. From 6 - 11 years old they attend primary school; from 11-15, they go to a college. Many then go to a secondary school, or *lycée* to study for the *baccalauréat* or to train for a job. The *"bac"* is a very tough exam–you have to pass it to go on to university. The school day often starts at 8:30 am and finishes at 5:30 pm. There is a two-hour break for lunch. Lessons last for 55 minutes each, with five minutes in between to get from one classroom to the next. Children often go to school on Saturday mornings too, although they have a day off on Wednesday.

anglais	8.30 - 9.25
français	9.30 - 10.25
sciences	10.30 - 11.25
mathématiques	11.30 - 12.25
Le déjeuner	12.30 - 2.30
histoire	2.30 - 3.25
géographie	3.30 - 4.25

KEEPING INFORMED

French people like to know what is happening in the world and enjoy discussing events. There are over 85 daily newspapers to choose from, including *Le Monde*, *Le Figaro*, and *France-Soir.* There are also magazines, such as *Paris-Match* and *L'Express.* The most popular magazine is *Télé 7 Jours,* a guide that tells people what's on television!

USEFUL SHOPS

France is famous for its hypermarkets–huge supermarkets where you can buy anything and everything. In contrast, there are the *Bar-Tabacs.* These are small bars that sell beer and wine, coffee, snacks, postage stamps, and bus or train tickets.

Say it in French
l'école - school
l'église - church
les devoirs - homework
le journal - newspaper
le travail - work
l'usine - factory
la maison - house

French Style

FRENCH FASHION

Paris is one of the fashion centers of the world. Each spring, French designers show their latest collections in Paris. They range from the classic style of Yves Saint Laurent to the more unusual designs of Jean-Paul Gaultier. Designers, models, fashion buyers, and fashion writers come from far and wide to see the shows. The Paris collection influences fashion all over the world and sets the trend for the year to come.

French *haute couture* (fashion) and perfumes are world-famous. Even the word *chic* is French!

The designs of Jean-Paul Gaultier are guaranteed to make an impression.

Classical elegance is the style set by Yves St. Laurent.

Lavender grows in plenty in the fields of Provence.

FRENCH PERFUMES

The major fashion houses also create and sell their own brands of perfumes. They include Dior, Chanel, and Givenchy. France has had a perfume industry since the sixteenth century. Grasse in southern France is the center of the industry. To create its perfumes, it uses locally grown wild lavender, jasmine, and violets and imported flowers such as roses, mimosa, and orange blossom.

Say it in French
les vêtements - clothes
la robe - dress
le chapeau - hat
les souliers - shoes
la fleur - flower
le parfum - perfume

Perfumed Jewelry

Try creating your own designer jewelry using perfumed petal beads.

YOU WILL NEED:

4 HANDFULS OF DRIED CHAMOMILE FLOWERS

SMALL SAUCEPAN

2 HANDFULS OF FRESH OR DRIED ROSE PETALS

NEEDLE THREADED WITH THIN BEAD THREAD

NECKLACE FASTENER

BLENDER OR FOOD PROCESSOR

1. Put the chamomile flowers and rose petals into the saucepan and add just enough water to cover them.

2. Ask an adult to heat the water to just below boiling point and let your ingredients simmer for an hour. Check the saucepan regularly to make sure that the water isn't boiling. If the water level drops, add more to just cover the petals.

3. After an hour, turn off the heat and pour your ingredients into the blender. Mix for a minute and then scoop the mixture out of the blender with a spatula.

4. Squeeze the mixture in your hands as hard as you can to get rid of any excess water.

5. Roll the mixture into beads and leave them somewhere warm to dry. This will take about three days.

6. When your beads are bone-dry, string them together. Push the needle through each bead very carefully, otherwise they will crack. (If you're feeling very artistic you could try adding other types of beads into your necklace as well.)

7. To finish, attach the ends of the bead thread to the fastener. If you knot the thread ends and fastener together, put a spot of glue on each knot to fix it in place.

When not in use, store your perfumed jewelry in an airtight box to help preserve its scent.

The World of Technology

France is a world leader in science and technology. It has a thriving car and aircraft industry and also uses its technological know-how in many other ways.

FRANCE ON THE MOVE

France is the fourth biggest car producer in the world, next to the United States, Japan, and Germany. Among its best-known cars are Renault, Peugeot, and Citroën. They are exported to many other countries. French car designers are always looking for new ideas and styles. One of the very latest Renault designs is an environmentally-friendly electric car.

The French railroad system, SNCF (*Société Nationale des Chemins de Fer*) prides itself on its fast, modern trains. The TGV (*Train à Grande Vitesse*) is the world's fastest passenger train, with an average speed of over 137 mph (220 km/h). The first TGV came into service in 1983. They now run between all the major cities in France.

Renault's latest creation, designed to be energy-saving, is the electric car. For easy parking, the rear wheels fold in.

FRANCE IN SPACE

France is a key member of the European Space Agency (ESA) that was founded in 1975. ESA's latest venture was to develop and build a mini space shuttle, called *Hermès*. It was to be launched by ESA's rocket, *Ariane*. The future of the project is now uncertain, however.

THE CHANNEL TUNNEL

The idea of an undersea tunnel linking Great Britain and France was first suggested in 1802. Work finally began on the Channel Tunnel in 1987 and it is due to be completed in the mid-1990s. Then, special trains will carry people, cars, and freight under the seabed from Folkestone in England to Calais in France. It is estimated that a journey from London to Paris will take just 3 1/4 hours.

THEME PARK MAGIC

French technology has also been put into action at two theme parks– EuroDisney, near Paris, and Futuroscope, near Poitiers. EuroDisney was opened in 1992. Thanks to lasers, video, computers, and other technological magic, visitors can explore four fantasy worlds and meet famous Disney characters such as Mickey and Goofy.

Futuroscope is another theme park that combines the latest technology with having fun. Here you can travel through space, explore the future, and sit in a theater where the seats move or where you are entirely surrounded by the screen.

Say it in French
la voiture - car
le train - train
l'avion - aircraft
l'espace - space
le voyage - journey
le métro - underground railway

French people enjoy sports and follow it closely. Some very famous sporting events take place each year in France.

LE MANS

Sports cars competing in the Le Mans 24-hour race drive all night and all day at speeds of over 250 mph (400 km/h).

SOCCER AND RUGBY

Soccer is the most popular team sport in France. The fortunes of the national team and of league teams, such as Marseille, are often the subject of heated discussions! The French rugby union team is one of the best in the world. Each year it competes in the Five Nations' Championship against England, Scotland, Wales, and Ireland.

TENNIS TOURNAMENT

The Roland Garros Stadium in Paris is the scene of the French Open tennis championship in May. This is one of the four Grand Slam tennis events alongside Wimbledon, the U.S. Open, and the Australian Open.

TOUR DE FRANCE

Each summer, over 100 professional cyclists take part in the Tour de France bicycle race. The race follows a 2,975-mile (4,800-km) course through France– the route changing each year. The riders race each day for about one month. Spectators line the route.

HORSE RACING

The *Prix de l'Arc de Triomphe* is one of the most famous and prestigious horse races in the world. It is run at the Longchamp racecourse in Paris.

Say it in French
le tennis - tennis
le football - football
le cheval - horse
l'équipe - team
le jeu - game
la course - race
la bicyclette - bicycle
le vélo - bicycle

Boules for Beginners

If you stroll through a village or town square in France on a summer's evening you will probably see a group of people playing *boules*. *Boules*, or *pétanque*, is the national game of France. It is played with metal balls and a jack ball. The object of the game is to toss or roll the *boules* as close to the jack as possible.

boule ○ *jack ball*

Boules is played between two teams of either one, two, or three players. Single players have three or four *boules* each. Players in teams of two have three *boules* each, and players in teams of three have two each.

1. To start, a player from team A draws a circle to stand in and throws the jack 18 - 30 feet (5.5 - 10 m) in front of them. Then they throw their first *boule* as close to the jack as possible. Their feet must stay inside the circle.

2. A player from team B then steps into the circle and tries to throw their *boule* closer to the jack or to knock the other *boule* away.

3. It is up to whichever team is not winning at this stage to keep throwing their *boules* until one lands nearest to the jack. Then it is the other team's turn. When a team has no *boules* left to play, the other team throws its remaining *boules*.

4. When neither team has any *boules* left, the score is added up. The team with the *boule* closest to the jack scores one point for each *boule* which is better placed than the opposing team's best *boule*. For example, if team A has two *boules* nearer to the jack than team B's best placed *boule*, team A scores two points.

5. At the end of each round, the winning team draws another circle, throws the jack, and starts a new round. The first team to reach 13 points is the winner.

Holidays and Festivals

The French have a wide variety of holidays and festivals including national holidays such as Christmas, saints' days, and local fairs and festivals.

HAPPY CHRISTMAS!

Christmas is celebrated in various ways in different parts of France. In Alsace and Lorraine, people put up and decorate Christmas trees. In Provence, they have a crib (*crèche*) with wooden nativity figures (*santons*). People do not usually give their presents on Christmas Day. They give them on St. Nicholas's Day (December 6) or on *la Fête des Rois* (January 6). A special cake is eaten on *la Fête des Rois*. It contains a bean or a tiny plastic figure. If you get the bean or figure in your piece of cake, you are king or queen for the day.

BASTILLE DAY

July 14 is a national holiday in France. It is the anniversary of the storming of the Bastille prison in Paris in 1789. This marked the start of the French Revolution. On Bastille Day there is a grand military procession in Paris, fireworks, and dancing.

FETES AND FESTIVALS

There are hundreds of local festivals all over France. Some celebrate saints' days. Others celebrate farming events such as the grape or lavender harvest, or local produce such as snails, cheese, and oysters. In Brittany, people celebrate festivals called *Pardons* to honor their local saints. They dress in traditional costume (right) and perform traditional folk dances.

EN VACANCES

French people are entitled to five weeks' vacation a year. They usually take time off in July and August. Then the roads are packed with people heading for the coast, the mountains, or the countryside.

MARDI GRAS

The town of Nice holds a huge carnival each year to mark the two weeks before Lent begins. The streets are filled with brightly decorated floats and people in fancy costumes. There are brass bands, fireworks, and flower battles.

FILM FESTIVAL

Each year in May, an international film festival is held in Cannes in the south of France. Famous film stars, directors, and producers come to see the latest films debut. Prizes are awarded to the best films and the best actors.

Say it in French
les vacances - vacation
la fête - festival
le Noël - Christmas
les Pâques - Easter
l'anniversaire - birthday

21

Make a Carnival Mask

YOU WILL NEED:

SEVEN SHEETS OF NEWSPAPER (TORN INTO LITTLE STRIPS)

FUNGICIDE-FREE WALLPAPER PASTE

4 lb. (1.75 KG) OF MODELING CLAY

WHITE PAPER GLUE

CLEAR HOUSEHOLD VARNISH

TAPE MEASURE

TAPE

PETROLEUM JELLY

CRÊPE PAPER

SANDPAPER

SCISSORS

MODELING TOOL

SMALL KITCHEN KNIFE

STAPLER

PAINTBRUSHES

PIPE CLEANERS

TOOTHPICK

THICK SEWING NEEDLE

PENCIL OR PEN

A STRIP OF WIDE ELASTIC

WHITE ACRYLIC PAINT

WATER-BASED PAINT

A WIPEABLE SURFACE TO WORK ON

To make the modeling clay mold

1. Hold the tape measure under your chin and measure all the way around your face. Make a note of this measurement.

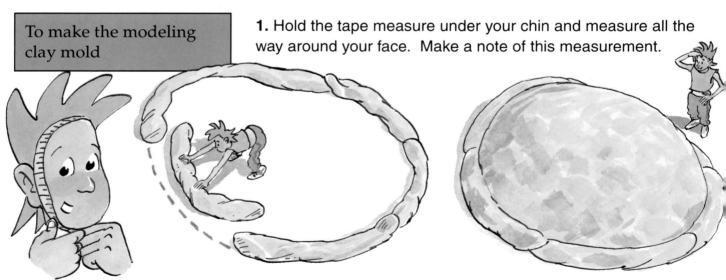

2. Knead the modeling clay to make it warm. Then roll some of it into sausages and use these to make the outline of a face. The circumference of this shape should be about the same as your face measurement.

3. Fill in the outline with small lumps of clay until it looks like a flat-topped mound.

22

4. Hold the clay mold against your face and carefully mark the position of your eyes and mouth. Using these markings as a guide, cut holes for your eyes and mouth with the knife. Shape and smooth the edges of these holes with the modeling tool.

5. Model a nose, chin, and cheeks from small lumps of clay and join them to the mold with the modeling tool. Use the modeling tool to carve eye sockets as well.

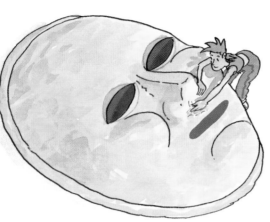 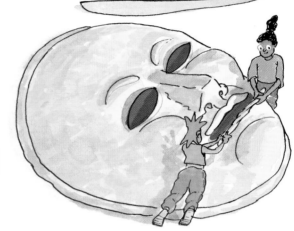

6. To make lips and eyelids, shape small lumps of clay into rolls and join them to the mold with the modeling tool.

To make the pâpier maché mask

7. Cover the surface of your mold with a layer of petroleum jelly. Now add a layer of newspaper strips dipped in the wallpaper paste. Wait for the glued paper to dry and add another layer. Your mask will need about seven layers in total. (Make sure that each layer is dried out completely before you apply the next one.)

8. When the final layer of paper is dry, ease the mask away from its mold. Gently rub it with sandpaper to make it smooth, and paint it with white acrylic paint. This acrylic undercoat will help your topcoat of paint stay bright.

9. Once the undercoat has dried, you can paint your mask any color you like. If you want your mask to have a shiny finish, cover it with a coat of clear gloss varnish once the paint has dried.

There are lots of ways to decorate your mask, but if you want to wear it for *un carnaval de Pâques* why not liven it up with some paper spring flowers?

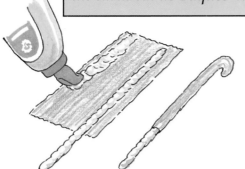  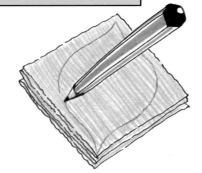

10. Glue a length of green crêpe paper around two-thirds of a pipe cleaner to make a stem. Bend the top of the pipe cleaner over into a small hook.

11. Cut a strip of crêpe paper into a fringe and wind it around the hooked end of the pipe cleaner. Secure the fringe to the stem with tape.

12. Fold some crêpe paper in half several times. Draw a petal shape and cut it out. You will have lots of identical petals which you can then tape onto your flower stem, one at a time.

13. When you've added as many petals as you need, glue a small rectangle of green crêpe paper around their base to cover the tape.

To attach each flower

14. Pierce the rim of your mask with the needle and widen the hole with the toothpick. Push your flower stem into the hole and tape it to the back of your mask. Make and secure more flowers in the same way.

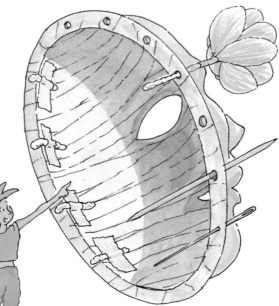

15. When your mask is complete, staple the strip of elastic to its sides, making sure that the jagged ends of each staple are on the outside. Now put on your mask and get set to celebrate.

24

If you want to add a frill or veil, cut a piece of lace or netting to the right length and attach it to the edges of your mask.

25

The Arts

French culture has produced many masterpieces of writing and art. Here you can find out about just a few of them.

Victor Hugo (1802 - 1850)

Paul Gauguin (1848 - 1903)

Auguste Rodin (1840 - 1917)

Molière (1622 - 1673)

Victor Hugo wrote poems, novels, and plays. His two most famous novels are *The Hunchback of Notre Dame* and *Les Misérables*. When he died in 1885, all of France went into mourning.

When Gauguin was 35 years old, he left his job as a stockbroker to become a painter. He later traveled to Tahiti where his work was inspired by the people and bright colors of the South Sea islands.

Molière wrote comedies based on people's weaknesses and odd behavior. For example, *Le Malade Imaginaire* is about a hypochondriac, and *Le Misanthrope* is about a man who didn't get along with anyone except himself.

One of Rodin's most famous sculptures is *The Thinker*. It is now on display in the Rodin Museum in Paris.

Say it in French
le livre - book
l'artiste - artist
la peinture - painting
l'écrivain - writer
le stylo - pen
le papier - paper

Dabs and Dashes

This painting, called *Impression, Sunrise*, was painted by Claude Monet. When it was first exhibited in Paris in 1874, alongside other paintings in a similar style, art critics threw up their hands in horror. This new style of painting was far too vague for their liking and so they nicknamed the artists "Impressionists."

Although invented as an insult to Monet and his colleagues, the term "Impressionism" suited their style of painting well. Unlike most artists at that time, the Impressionists were more interested in capturing the atmosphere of a scene than portraying a lifelike image of it. In particular, they wanted to show how sunlight affects the color and shape of an object. To achieve this, they painted in dabs and dashes, avoiding neat outlines, and mixed the colors on their canvases rather than on their palettes.

One of the quickest ways to capture an impression of a scene is to paint it onto dampened white paper. Choose an outdoor scene that looks interesting in the sunlight and find a comfortable spot from which to paint it. When you've decided which colors you are going to use, brush some clean water over your paper and apply your paint quickly in dabs. The wetter your paper, the farther your paint will flow. If part of your paper dries out before you can paint on it, just wet it again. Be careful, as wet paper is very fragile and will tear easily.

If you can, go back to your chosen scene at a different time of the day and paint it again. The change in sunlight should give you a whole new set of colors and shadows to paint.

French History

France is an old country with a long and sometimes turbulent history. Here are some of the key events and characters.

THE ROMANS

Julius Caesar and his Roman army conquered France in 58 B.C. The country was known as Gaul. There are many Roman remains in France, including amphitheaters and aqueducts. The Roman conquest also inspired the later adventures of the cartoon character *Astérix*. His village holds out against the Romans, thanks to a magic potion that gives the villagers superhuman strength!

THE NORMAN CONQUEST

In A.D. 895, Normandy in northern France was invaded by Vikings from Norway and Denmark. They became known as the Normans. The Norman king, William (the Conqueror), defeated the English king, Harold, at the Battle of Hastings in 1066 and became king of England.

JOAN OF ARC

When she was a young girl, Joan of Arc (Jeanne d'Arc) heard the voice of God telling her to save France and restore the French king to his rightful throne. At that time, France was under English rule. Joan obeyed and in 1429 led the French army to victory at the town of Orléans. The following year, however, she was taken prisoner by the English and later burned at the stake. The Roman Catholic church made her into a saint in 1920.

VIVE LA REVOLUTION!

On July 14, 1789, the Bastille prison in Paris was stormed by ordinary French people. They were tired of being hungry and poor while the French king lived in luxury. The French Revolution had begun. The king, Louis XVI, his queen, Marie Antoinette, and many other royal and noble people were sent to the guillotine. France became a republic.

NAPOLEON BONAPARTE

Napoléon Bonaparte (1769-1821) was a brilliant army general who had himself crowned emperor of France in 1804. He was eventually defeated by the Duke of Wellington at the Battle of Waterloo in 1815. He was sent into exile on the island of St. Helena in the South Atlantic. He died there in 1821. His remains now lie in the *Hôtel des Invalides* in Paris.

GENERAL DE GAULLE

During World War II, Charles de Gaulle (1890-1970) was the leader of the Free French, or French Resistance, against the Nazis. In 1958, he became the first president of the Fifth Republic in France. He negotiated the independence of Algeria from France in 1962 and had a great influence on French politics. He resigned in 1969.

Say it in French
l'histoire - history
le roi - king
le soldat - soldier
la bataille - battle
le président - president
la politique - politics

TIME BAND

58 B.C. Romans invade France

A.D.486 Roman Empire collapses; Franks conquer

A.D.768 - 814 Reign of Charlemagne

A.D.895 Vikings settle in Normandy

1337 - 1453 Hundred Years War between France and England

1431 Jeanne d'Arc is burned at the stake in Rouen

1643 - 1715 Reign of Louis XIV, the Sun King

1789 - 1792 French Revolution

1792 The First Republic

1799 Napoléon comes to power

1815 Napoléon is defeated at the Battle of Waterloo

1848 - 1852 The Second Republic

1871 - 1946 The Third Republic

1914 - 1918 World War I

1939 - 1945 World War II

1940 - 1944 Germany occupies France

1946 - 1958 The Fourth Republic

1958 - present The Fifth Republic

Picture Pairs

Play Picture Pairs and see how many of the French words in this book you actually remember! The instructions given here are for two to four players, but as your French vocabulary increases, you might like to make more cards and include more players.

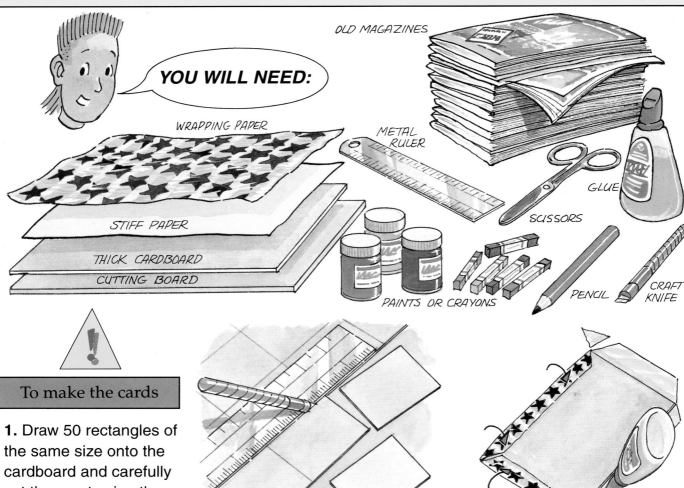

YOU WILL NEED:

OLD MAGAZINES

WRAPPING PAPER

METAL RULER

GLUE

SCISSORS

STIFF PAPER

THICK CARDBOARD

CUTTING BOARD

PAINTS OR CRAYONS

PENCIL

CRAFT KNIFE

To make the cards

1. Draw 50 rectangles of the same size onto the cardboard and carefully cut them out using the craft knife.

2. Draw another 50 rectangles onto the wrapping paper and cut them out too. These rectangles should be about $3/4$ inch (2 cm) longer and wider than the cardboard ones.

3. Cut the the corners of the paper rectangles as shown and glue them onto your cards.

4. Draw 25 rectangles, slightly smaller than your cards, onto the stiff paper and cut them out.

5. Choose 25 French words from this book and write them down with their English translations. (Keep this list beside you as you play the game.)

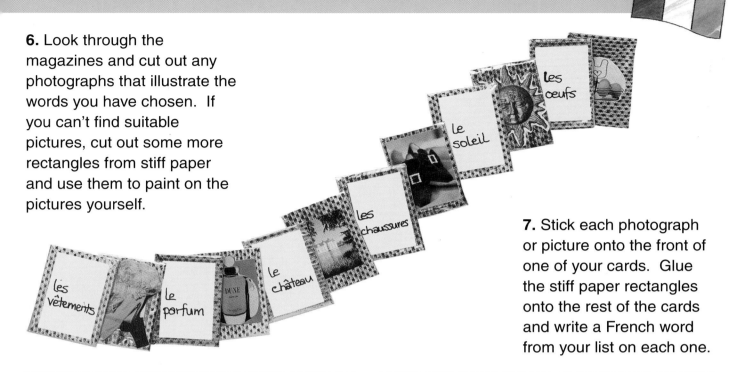

6. Look through the magazines and cut out any photographs that illustrate the words you have chosen. If you can't find suitable pictures, cut out some more rectangles from stiff paper and use them to paint on the pictures yourself.

les vêtements

le parfum

le château

les chaussures

le soleil

les œufs

7. Stick each photograph or picture onto the front of one of your cards. Glue the stiff paper rectangles onto the rest of the cards and write a French word from your list on each one.

To play the game
The object of Picture Pairs is to collect pairs of cards made up of words and their matching picture.

Each player starts the game with seven cards. The rest of the deck is placed face-down on the table. If you have any pairs, put them on the table in front of you.

Then ask one of the other players if he/she has a card that you need to make a pair. If that player has the card requested, he/she must hand it over and you win the pair and take another turn. If he/she does not have the card, you take a card from the deck in the middle and the turn passes to the next person.

All word cards must be translated into English. If you cannot remember the translation of the word, look it up and miss your next go.

The player who pairs all his/her cards first is the winner.

31

Index

Additional photographs:
Bridgeman Art Library 29; David Simpson 7(R); Eye Ubiquitous/© Jason Burke 7(T),
© F. Torrance 13(B), 28(T); Frank Spooner 4, 17(L), 18, 20(C), 21(R); J. Allen Cash 20(B), 21(B);
Renault 16(T); Rex Features 14(C),(R); Robert Harding Picture Library 12(R), 28(C); Zefa
Picture Library 6(BOTH), 7(B), 9, 12(L), 14(L), 16(B), 17(R); Visual Arts Library 26, 27.

Steven Holl

heart

Steven Holl

heart

HATJE CANTZ

This book has been published
with support from:

Realdania
The Obel Family Foundation

Contents

heart

Holger Reenberg

The Competition 1

When, in the spring of 2005, I first entered the room at Herning Kunstmuseum that displayed the anonymous boards of competition proposals for the new museum, one in particular caught my attention and would not let it go. In the months to come that room, known as the Stone Room, would house the thirteen-person committee charged with selecting the appropriate proposal for a new home for Herning Kunstmuseum.

The proposal that exercised such particular attraction for me was all in black and white and quite clearly handmade! By this I mean that the images of the building were not three-dimensional visualizations made with computer technology, but physical in nature, as in depicting an actual model. The images on the boards were alternately photographs of an architectural model, drawings made by hand, and watercolors. Indeed, one could claim, with just a hint of irony, that this was an art historian's dream of a presentation, but that was by no means all it had to commend itself. The boards evoked a range of formal and material allusions to the specific site, to history, and to art.

Damgaard, Gadegaard, and Manzoni

Since its inauguration in 1977, Herning Kunstmuseum had been housed in the Angli building, the shirt factory built by Aage Damgaard. At that time, the Damgaard family's Midtjysk Skole-og Kulturfond (Central Jutland Foundation for Education and Culture) had already donated the highlights from Aage Damgaard's extraordinary art collection to the Danish state with the aim of founding a state-recognized museum. Aage Damgaard had thus manufactured shirts on the premises that would later house Herning Kunstmuseum. At his shirt factory he established an approach to fostering cooperation between the business community and artists that was, and still remains, quite unique within a Danish context.

This sort of cooperation also forms the historical and conceptual basis for the Socle du Monde Biennial, which opened its doors in 2002 and is operated by HEART in conjunction with the local business council, Erhvervsrådet.

In a letter that Piero Manzoni wrote to a friend in the summer of 1960, penned on the stationary of the local Herning Missionshotel, he states that he had been employed by the Angli factory and given an assistant with a car. Aage Damgaard's attention had been called to Manzoni by the painter Paul Gadegaard. At the time, Gadegaard himself was busily working on decorating Damgaard's new factory building, known as The Black Factory. Indeed, the building's façade was pitch black, but inside all of its floors, walls, and ceilings were painted in bright, clear colors and abstract shapes. Gadegaard had been given free rein to create a total interior, a decorative art scheme on a previously unseen scale. It could be said that the dream of having art conquer the social realm, a dream entertained by an entire generation, reached its acme with Gadegaard's work in Herning during the period between 1952 and 1982.

Manzoni returned to Herning for another visit the following summer of 1961, and was again granted liberty to pursue the artistic goals of his own devising. As a result, Herning Kunstmuseum now owns thirty-seven works by Piero Manzoni, including *La Linea Lunga* (1960) and *Socle du Monde* (1961).

The operation of Herning Kunstmuseum has two pivotal points. One is the collection of works by Piero Manzoni. The largest public collection of its kind in the world, it attracts requests for loans from museums worldwide throughout any given year. The second pivotal point concerns the starting point of the permanent collection, that is, the private collection of the shirt manufacturer Aage Damgaard, and the unique way in which this collection was founded. Over the course of the last seven years the museum has sought to leverage these two pivotal points by having the Manzoni collection and Aage Damgaard's unique vein of patronage form part of the concept in connection with all of its events and exhibitions.

When it comes to loaning Manzoni's works to other institutions, the museum had never been able to organize exhibitions based on return loans, primarily because the physical properties of its setting—an old factory building—made it unsuitable as an exhibition venue. This is to say that the museum had been unable to organize exhibitions that match the quality of the collection it owns. When the museum lent works by Manzoni to the Guggenheim Museum in New York, for example, it was unable to accept the Guggenheim's offer of a corresponding loan from its collection of works by Wassily Kandinsky.

The Competition 2

This story, and this piece of art history, was immediately, yet elusively, evoked by the black and white boards in the Stone Room. The proposal's unmistakable focus on what Knud W. Jensen, founder of the Louisiana Museum of Modern Art in Denmark, called the "genius loci" or "spirit of place" was not achieved through some clever architectural metaphor or a directly symbolic shape, even though symbolism and metaphors were significant elements of the whole. In a manner of speaking, the building seemed to be conjuring up itself as a natural continuation of its concrete surroundings. At the same time, it combined a distinct functionality, matching the exhibition requirements with a poetic sense of the art that the building would house. What I did not know then, but perhaps should have been able to conjecture, was that the architect's name was Steven Holl.

I had a certain level of familiarity with Steven Holl's architecture from my days at the Arken Museum of Modern Art in Copenhagen. In my position at that museum, I had often entered into dialogue with Tuula Arkio and Maretta Jaukuuri, then director and chief curator of the Kiasma Museum of Contemporary Art in Helsinki, a building designed by Holl. I heard about their cooperation with the architect and also visited the site to witness the progress of the project, which combined great functionality and a respect for art with an expressive architectural idiom. After my arrival in Herning, Holl's name would crop up again in my conversations with Lars Damgaard.

The competition was announced on February 16, 2005. It was agreed that a total of six architects would be able to participate, four of which would be selected through prequalification rounds while the last two would be invited to submit proposals. The final field of contestants was comprised of CUBO and 3XNielsen—both from Aarhus in Denmark—along with Snøhetta of Oslo and Keith Williams Architects of London, whereas Steven Holl Architects of New York and Caruso St John of London were both specially invited to participate. It was a marvelous feeling to finally have reached the stage where an actual competition period (May 30 to September 9, 2005) could commence, given that we were awaiting contributions from such strong architects. Very importantly, it was incredibly satisfying for us to have found a supporter in The Foundation Realdania that believed in our project—and would back it financially. At that point I had been director of Herning Kunstmuseum for four years, with my overarching task being to bring about a new museum building.

2001–2005

In 2000 I was approached by Lars Damgaard, the new chairman of the board of directors at Herning Kunstmuseum and son of Aage Damgaard. Lars Damgaard was also the director of the restaurant chain A Hereford Beefstouw, which had been founded by his father. The meeting was a quick one, and Lars Damgaard's wishes were unequivocal: Herning Kunstmuseum was to start over, and it was to take place in a new building! Rounds of job interviews with the board of directors followed in rapid succession, and by March 2001 I started my new job as museum director at Herning. If a building project such as Steven Holl's design is ever to be realized in a provincial town, the moment needs to be exactly right. One could, however, be forgiven for showing a little local patriotism by asking whether every moment isn't exactly right in Herning. This is because Herning is well known for its entrepreneurial spirit, its initiative, and, quite prominently, its ability to cooperate across political and professional boundaries to achieve great results—results that would otherwise be beyond the reach of a small Danish town. Nevertheless, this challenge called for something special. The museum had attempted to realize a new building project twice before, but without success.

Before my arrival the project was already poised for a good start. Johannes Jensen, the (now sadly deceased) founder and manager of the local carpet company Wilton Tæpper, had given the Municipality of Herning a plot of land with the firm condition that it was to be used for a new art museum. What is more, the museum's board of directors had been given an infusion of new blood with the addition of new members.

Right from the outset Lars Damgaard; Johannes Poulsen, a member of the Danish parliament and the local city council; and I entered into a close, fruitful collaboration. In 2002 Lars Krarup became the new mayor of Herning, and his great commitment to the cause had a crucial impact on the completion of the project.

The year 2002 saw a number of preliminary contacts and decisions being made. That year set the course for the project, which would turn out to be the right one. Together with the Erhvervsrådet, Herning Kunstmuseum launched the Socle du Monde. The biennial is based on forging a cooperation between artists and the business community, all very much in the spirit of Aage Damgaard, that is, characterized by complete artistic freedom. Around the same time, the Municipality of Herning and the museum agreed to let the newly established regional orchestra, the MidWest Ensemble, have a residency in the new museum, should it ever be realized.

We also initiated contact with Henning Kruse Petersen, then the group president of the financial institute Nykredit. Kruse Petersen would later become chairman of the board of governors charged with raising funds for the building project. Kruse Petersen brought his wide-ranging network and a new dynamic to bear on the process. Most importantly, we set up our first meetings with the Realdania Foundation, piquing their interest sufficiently for them to decide on funding a survey, conducted by PLS Rambøll, to assess the feasibility of the project. Rambøll delivered its report, which proved positive, in early 2004, stating among other things that the most important precondition governing the success of the project was the Manzoni collection at Herning Kunstmuseum. On the basis of that report, Realdania decided to grant the funds required to hold an architectural competition.

HEART

There is architecture that works well on a screen or a canvas but should never make its way to an actual building site; and then there is architecture that is designed by people for people and the world. Over the last two decades we have witnessed the construction of many new art museums whose architecture may be interesting in itself, but is entirely unsuitable for an art museum or even an exhibition venue. Of course, this is to some extent a matter of taste; it all depends on what kind of museum we want, what role it should perform, and how we wish to present the art.

When we hear curators and museum directors speak of "the white cube," of the anonymous, flexible, square space as the only ideal solution for exhibition spaces, we sense an underlying wish that museum architecture should not change or develop. The need for an anonymous exhibition space is partly associated with the concept of art as autonomous and partly a need for spatial flexibility. The very expression "autonomous work of art" denotes a mode of perception that claims that art has a unique quality, something that is above and beyond virtually everything else. In a manner of speaking, this view posits that a masterpiece can be appreciated and recognized as a masterpiece entirely independently of all external factors. This is, of course, not true—not entirely, anyway!

This is because any given work can go unrecognized as art by anyone. Suffice it to say that recognizing this fact is an important parameter determining an art museum's opportunities for entering into a dialogue with its audience. If the meaning of a work of art depends on so many factors during its processes of creation, perception, and recognition, why should it not be dependent on the space? And, if this is true, why should it always depend on a white, anonymous space, which would, if taken to its logical conclusion, end up as a kind of global corporate identity?

As far as I can see, the discussion concerning the autonomous work of art as well as exhibition space need not be a question of either/or. Art museums can be created in churches, villages, on remote beaches, in malls, or in mountain passes, and we can exhibit whatever we wish in them. On the one hand, we must recognize that today, the interior and exterior of the museum take part in a forceful, contradictory dialogue with the society surrounding the building. That challenge must be faced, together with the many social benefits—and risks of contaminating the museum's core—that it entails. On the other hand, we could claim that some of the works that find their way to a museum—which is and should remain an historical institution—have achieved a certain degree of independent life, a kind of unassailable status, at least for a while. Within that time span and that space, we can occasionally experiment with isolating the works from the current agendas of consumer society and politics.

In the program for the competition we called the new museum "the open treasure box." We envisioned a house with a periphery that is open and inviting, while its inner chambers house true treasure boxes, offsetting the openness outside. Finding the right winner became a long and at times difficult task, but on October 14, 2005 we were able to announce the winner: Steven Holl's project. The ground breaking took place on June 25, 2007.

When the winner of the competition was announced, the professor and landscape architect Steen Høyer made the following comment in the Danish architect's journal *Arkitekten*:

> Today, it is rare to see a talented architect taking himself and his task seriously without letting the project be colored by showing-off or commercial detours ... The building owner wishes to secure a sense of seriousness in relation to the art .... [he wants a] firm, expressive framework which stands up for itself without being an aggressive or clever opponent ... Most architects view art as a commodity that can form part of the democratic landscape on standard market conditions. By contrast, this building owner wishes to retain the uniqueness of the works of art with a dignified building in Birk.

Now, each end of Birk Centerpark in Herning is home to a structure with strong sculptural qualities, but with crucial differences. One of them is Ingvar Cronhammar's sculpture *Elia,* inaugurated in 2001: the work of a mystic without reason or objective, negating and cancelling out the useful endeavors of the white business park. The other structure is Steven Holl's new—and yes, white—museum building called HEART, whose name and brilliant typeface was created by Kontrapunkt in 2007.

Like all his buildings, Steven Holl's HEART was created for its specific site, in this case with the objective of serving as a museum. The associations and references that I instinctively perceived on

Steven Holl Architects
View from the northeast / Model / HEART

my first encounter with the competition boards were initially communicated by the façades, with their appropriated functional geometry and the anthropomorphic expressiveness of the roof structure. The building's relationship between the organic and the geometric acts as a paraphrase of the concrete art of Paul Gadegaard, whose point of departure seems to have been the leftover fabric from the shirt manufactory at Angli.

The theme of HEART concerns tactility and materiality. The external walls were molded on-site, created in white concrete, and the façades greet us with a crumpled, textile-like surface. These tactile (and textile) references are continued in the roof, which governs the floor plan. The roof is made up of five shells reminiscent of shirtsleeves cut lengthwise. The sleeves evoke strong allusions to the raised shells of the nearby prototype house of Jørn Utzon. With its light, crumpled walls and hanging sleeves, HEART has the effect of a tent made of concrete.

The sleeve-like roof structure also encompasses two recessed flat roofs. The sleeves and surfaces are joined by a vertical band of sand-blasted glass canals providing the exhibition rooms with light.

The crucial core of the floor plan is its two exhibition spaces; their perpendicular linearity plays against the organic feel of the ceilings. The governing concept of the floor plan—having the exhibition spaces form rectangular and square cubes within a "covered square," surrounded by the other functions within the outer shell of the building—complies with the competition program's stipulations regarding a general openness combined with the idea of the "treasure box."

The language of HEART is not an authoritarian architectural idiom applied arbitrarily in order to create a place apart, a place where economy, politics, and lifestyle are or become the crucial parameters. Rather, the building is shaped to relate partly to its neighbors—the Utzon house and the Angli factory—and partly to the history that shaped the place and unique art collection, of which HEART is the connecting arc.

Piero Manzoni
Achrome, 1960 / HEART

monochrome

Steven Holl

Nemchinovka

As it was our first trip to Moscow, we wanted to visit Kazimir Malevich's grave marker—a white cube with a black square—which we had seen in photographs. In an e-mail exchange with our friends, the architects Ludmilla and Vladimir Kirpichev, the latter of whom is also a professor, we asked them to include this in our itinerary. Ludmilla explained that the marker, along with the huge oak tree it was under, was destroyed during World War II. She wrote: "to go to Nemchinovka is to go nowhere . . . ," to which my wife, the artist Solange Fabião, immediately replied: " . . . then we must go there!"

It had been obsessed with the work of Malevich since the mid seventies, when I discovered his *White on White* (1918) and *Black Square* (1915) paintings and his Suprematist Manifesto writings. For four years after arriving in New York in 1977 all of the drawings I made were black and white. Solange had been obsessed with Malevich since her years in Berlin at the Akademie der Künste (University of the Arts) and Freie Universität from 1986 to 1988.

It was a sunny March morning when the two of us set out from Moscow in a rental car, driving toward Nemchinovka. Under a crisp blue sky there were patches of snow. After driving for several hours we reached a scattering of fairly recently built dachas (summer houses), where we discovered a street named "Malevich." We turned down a road lined with melted snow and shortly arrived at a clearing. There was a large white cube with a red square on which was written: " . . . here is the location of my father's grave as I remember it . . . " The reconstructed cube was set by Malevich's daughter in 1989, the year before she died. Vladimir and Ludmilla stood in disbelief while Solange and I were thrilled to discover this site in Nemchinovka. Later we found the green wooden dacha that Malevich had used in the summer marked with a bronze plaque.

Monochrome, Achrome, Malevich & Manzoni

Thinking of the forty-six original works by Piero Manzoni in the HEART Herning Museum of Contemporary Art in Herning, Denmark, we could look back; from Malevich's monochrome obsessions and writings there is a spiritual bridge to Piero Manzoni's achrome works.

Steven Holl Architects
View from the northwest / HEART

Holger Reenberg has written about the links between Malevich and Manzoni, who wanted "to reach the zero point from where anything is possible . . ." Although I was familiar with Piero Manzoni, I first discovered that he had created many of his most important works in Herning, Denmark while reading the extended booklet produced for the competition for the Herning Center of the Arts. This site in the center of Denmark's Jutland Peninsula seemed charged with the mysterious energy of 1960s Arte Povera, Gruppo Zero, and the monochromatic desert ground of Malevich.

We were among six architects invited to compete for the new Herning Center of the Arts, which was to be sited near the former shirt factory now occupied by the museum. The plan of this 1960s building was made in the shape of a shirt collar . . . Herning was an interesting, idiosyncratic place. While we had received the competition brief and booklet in April or May, we delayed working on the competition due to the number of other works and competitions in the office. (That summer of 2005 we had won three competitions in a row, including the Knokke-Heist Hotel in Belgium and the Cité de l'Océan et du Surf in Biarritz with Solange Fabião.) In late August, I reread the competition brief and enthusiastically accepted the proposed building constraints, which included a height limit of eight meters and the color white.

I studied Piero Manzoni's work at length as a way into the competition. The *Socle du Monde* (1961) had inspired me years before, when studying the work of Robert Smithson, Michael Heizer, and other conceptually focused artists working with land. Piero Manzoni had preceded them all with *Socle du Monde,* which was crafted at the Angli Factory. Many fabric explorations in his achrome series had also been made at Herning. As a connection to these works, we imaged the building in white tilt-up concrete with the forms lined to suggest the texture of wrinkled fabric.

Steven Holl Architects
Watercolor / HEART

Steven Holl Architects
South elevation / Drawing / HEART

It was a coincidence to discover that my favorite Danish architect, Jørn Utzon, had built one of his prototypical buildings of 1972 next to the museum site. Occupied now as a residence and beautifully maintained, its relation to the new building was important in our initial thinking.

Treasure Boxes / Shirtsleeves

With a little more than a week left, I spent the weekend making sketches toward a concept. I decided to envision the galleries as two "treasure boxes"—rectangles at the center of the plan, which would then have loosely displaced curvilinear, light-gathering roof elements. The flat, featureless landscape was partially echoed in the reverse-curve of the roof's geometry, fusing the architecture and the landscape. From the air the forms resembled shirtsleeves thrown onto boxes. The loose edges of the plan could be adjusted for the café, auditorium, and lobby, and the orthogonal exhibition spaces could be accessed separately for after-hours use of the facility. Located on a single level, the building would have excellent circulation and be geothermally heated and cooled.

Clearly anchored to the site of the building, this seemed an inspired concept. The interior spaces would come alive with a gradually curved light. Monday morning I returned to the office with the sketches and asked three assistants if they could produce the presentation in the week left before the deadline. After they enthusiastically replied, "Yes!," several all-night work sessions got us to the deadline—the presentation boards with black and white photos of the little model looked stunning. I imagined an amazing quality of light within the orthogonal walls of the galleries. The cliché complaints about new art museums today revolve around their being either too expressive for good gallery space or, at the other extreme, a collection of white boxes that suck the life out of art. We had devised a third way. The entire presentation—all seven boards—was limited to black and white.

Scandinavian Blood / Northern Light

My grandfather was born in Tønsberg, Norway. My father, a full-blooded Norwegian, raised us on the edge of Puget Sound near Seattle. The low angle of northern sunlight there in the winter has a special inspiring power similar to that of Scandinavia. In 1993, we were invited to compete for the Museum of Contemporary Art in Helsinki. The concept of intertwining northern light, the fabric of the city, and the landscape in our scheme "Kiasma" prevailed, as our project was selected over 516 other entries. To highlight the low angle of Helsinki sunlight, a "light catching" section was developed. We are currently completing the Knut Hamsun Center above the Arctic Circle in Hamarøy, Norway. Here the northern light conditions are extreme, with six weeks of midnight sun in the summer and no sun at all in January.

These building experiences and my Scandinavian blood gave me a head start in conceiving the Herning building with a special quality of light connecting it to its site. The curved "shirtsleeve"-like roofs turn upward with strips of skylights to catch the low angle of the sun and allow it to slightly grace across the downward curving ceiling. The geometry of the light-reflecting curves distributes the light so wonderfully in the gallery spaces that they can be used without artificial light. The space is animated and alive when a cloud moves in front of, or away from, the sun—as often happens in this region.

Planar Architecture / Fabric Forms

The planar nature of the curved roof elements draped over the treasure boxes of the galleries was followed by the planar development of other spaces in white concrete. Truck tarps were inserted into the concrete formwork, yielding a fabric texture that swallows the imperfections of rapid construction. Floors of integral-color charcoal concrete unify the ground plane into a continuous patina with a wax finish. Diffused light in areas like the café was achieved by using sandblasted channel glass. Earth mounds, which extend the geometry of the building into the landscape, form spaces around the museum; at the entrance, a curved mound forms a space protecting it from the adjacent highway.

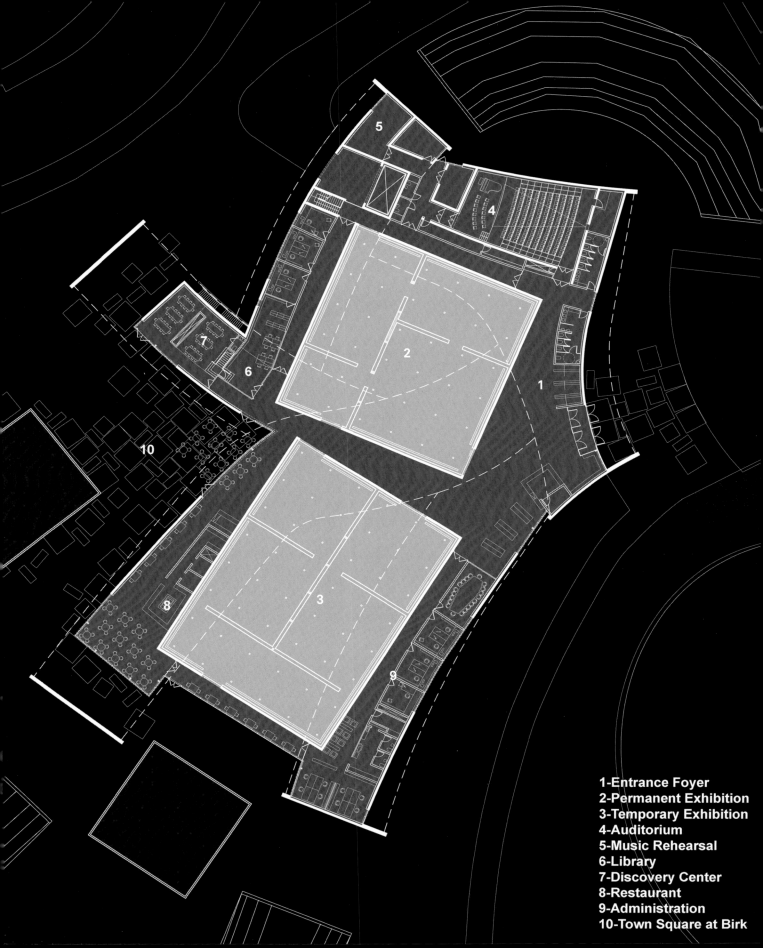

1-Entrance Foyer
2-Permanent Exhibition
3-Temporary Exhibition
4-Auditorium
5-Music Rehearsal
6-Library
7-Discovery Center
8-Restaurant
9-Administration
10-Town Square at Birk

On the south side, large reflecting pools gather and reflect the sunlight onto soffits. The landscape architect Torben Schønherr has developed our competition concept with his own delicate porous paving and plantings.

Halloween Phone Call

After we had just made the deadline for sending out the boards, we turned to another project and forgot about the competition. Then, on October 31st—Halloween—I received a phone call from Herning Museum director Holger Reenberg, who announced "Steven, you've won the competition! We want to build this [design] and move within two years!" Coming from Copenhagen, the call was innocent of its implication arriving on Halloween, which in New York is a day of fear mixed with joy.

Realization: Luminist Space of Surprise

Questions of Perception, which I wrote together with Juhani Pallasmaa and Alberto Pérez-Gómez in 1994, has a chapter titled "Perspective Space: Incomplete Perception." It argues that our perception of space develops from a series of overlapping perspectives, which unfold according to the angle of speed and movement. Although we might analyze our movement along a specific path at a given speed, we can never enumerate all possible views.

The Herning building is a physical embodiment of these ideas. Rather than a building experienced first as an object, it offers a series of exterior experiences fused with the landscape. As we move around the exterior of the building, we experience very different spaces, none of which add up to an object or a singularity. Going into the building is quite a different experience. There is a sense of surprise on entering, especially if we enter at the end of the day around half past five in the afternoon, when the low angle of the western sun seems to blow through the two low slung curves capturing the light at the ceiling.

As one moves forward through the splayed rectilinear walls containing the galleries, the spaces glide into one or the other, where the glowing curve of the ceiling follows a direction of flow through a sequence of spaces. The gallery spaces, where the walls always meet the floors at right angles, are shaped to focus attention on the art, whereas those at the perimeter of the building become more fuzzy, interacting with the landscape. The café spaces, for instance, spill out onto terraces. The Concert Hall for the MidWest Ensemble opens onto its own practice rooms and service space while connecting to the main lobby. The galleries at the center of the building can be easily closed while all the peripheral spaces remain open for after-hours use. The monochrome framework of the architecture foregrounds the color of the art, which charges the space differently according to each artist and each exhibition. The rectilinear spaces of the galleries have been fine-tuned according to the ratio of 1:1.618—as in all our projects. In his seminal book, *The Geometry of Art and Life* (1946), Matila Ghyka puts forth an argument for proportion based on mathematical principles found in nature; the Golden Section ratio 1:1.618 is the key ratio in organic growth.

As we walk through the spaces connecting the administrative offices, the presence of the curved planar roofs above again energizes the space, but in an upward swinging curve toward the landscape outside. For all those who work in this museum, the planar and light-catching geometry of the architecture will enliven the everyday tasks and activities within and outward into the landscape. The monochromatic frame of the museum architecture is animated by the changing light angles, every day and throughout the seasons. With the building's Concert Space, which can act as an events auditorium, as well as its Children's Center, restaurant, and outdoor gathering areas, the hope is for the museum to act as a social condenser for the community. The core of the museum—the galleries—aims at a "luminist" space for changing art.

Upon his first encounter with the spaces, the artist Jannis Kounellis said they remind him of sheds with hanging fisherman's nets. Perhaps here one can read a bit of the ocean in the continuous flatland site of the Jutland Peninsula—a swelling of landscape turning into waves of light, marking a "zero point" as Piero Manzoni said . . . "where anything is possible."

Steven Holl Architects
Foyer / HEART

Steven Holl Architects
View from the northwest / Model / HEART

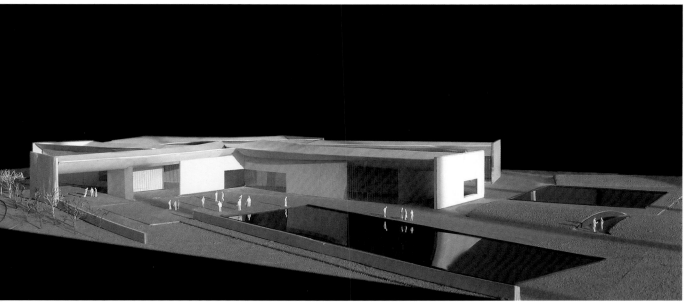

HEART
HERNING MUSEUM
OF CONTEMPORARY ART

heart

HEART / Foyer

HEART / Foyer

HEART / View from the southwest

HEART / Detail of façade

HEART / View from the south

HEART / View from the west

HEART / View from the southwest

HEART
Detail / Café exterior

HEART / Educational Center

HEART / Office

HEART / Hallway
between exhibition spaces 1 and 2

HEART / Exhibition space 2

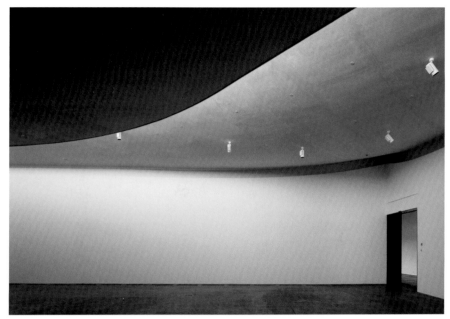

HEART / Exhibition space 2

HEART / Exhibition space 2

facade

HEART / Concert hall

HEART / Detail of Concert hall

Lucio Fontana
Concetto Spaziale, Attese, 1967 / HEART

thought and phenomena

Juhani Pallasmaa

Architectural thought is the working through of phenomena initiated by idea. By "making" we realize idea is only a seed for extension in phenomena.
—Steven Holl, *Anchoring*

Steven Holl's architectural trajectory from the early projects of the mid-1970s, which reflected the air of contemporaneous Italian Rationalism, to the relaxed and experientially multifaceted HEART Herning Museum of Contemporary Art, which will be inaugurated this year, is long and surprising. The twenty-five years separating these polar phases of his career seem to fuse more than a lifetime of intense creative exploration in the formal, perceptual, and mental essences of the art of building. His journey as a designer has been guided by tireless reading in poetry (including poets like Osip Mandelstam, Anna Ahmatova, and Paul Celan in addition to others writing in English), philosophy, and scientific literature as well as by his deep engagement in the world of the visual arts. The scope of his design work is impressively varied at the same time that it is determined and consistent, as if having followed a preconceived plan. As this path has meandered and branched off into new directions, it has also gradually and convincingly established the singular and recognizable world of Steven Holl, the architect. That he was very recently granted the unique *Frontiers of Knowledge Award in the Arts,* sponsored by the Spanish BBVA Bank, underlines the fact that he has reached the highest international level of architectural esteem. Indeed, during the past two decades he has also been one of the most inspiring role models and idols in architectural education around the world. His open-minded sense of curiosity and his rare capacity to fuse creative design with philosophical clarity and poetic literary expression have reinforced his impact in the world of architectural education.

The artistic universes of architects and artists tend to become increasingly idiosyncratic, narrow, and hermetic over time as a consequence of a conscious quest for an identifiable artistic identity. Holl's world, by contrast, has continually opened up to new influences, aspirations, and architectural solutions. His buildings are not variations on established architectural anatomies or his own prior architectural themes; they tend to be new architectural typologies and spatial experiences. His early interest in architectural typologies remerged later on in his continued aspiration to generate novel architectural types—new architectural creatures, as it were. He seems to inject a novel architectural DNA, so to speak, into each new commission and to create an unforeseen specimen of architecture in each new task. Just think of the dramatic differences between, say, the labyrinthine scheme for the Palazzo del Cinema in Venice (1990), somewhat reminiscent of the folds of the human brain; the ensemble of sculpted and modulated light in the Chapel of St. Ignatius at Seattle University (1994–97); the gigantic porous urban wall and the constructed caves of the Simmons Hall dormitories at the Massachusetts Institute of Technology in Cambridge (1992–2002); the silvery extruded sectional shape of the Whitney Water Purification Facility and Park in Connecticut (1998–2005), suggesting images of the life-giving purity of water; and the illuminated glass plank lanterns, or "lenses," of the Nelson-Atkins Museum of Art in Kansas City (1999–2007), rising authoritatively from the earth. Regardless of his interest in integrated and sculpted spaces and forms, Holl occasionally creates projects that are based on a strict orthogonal geometry and simple tectonic language, such as the Swiss Residence in Washington D.C. (2001–06), the Writing with Light House on Long Island (2001–04), and the Planar House in Paradise Valley, Arizona (2002–05).

Like all architects, Holl began his career with small theoretical projects, shop interiors, renovations, and houses, but he has also recently executed enormous urban projects, such as the Makuhari Housing project in Chiba, Japan (1992–96); the Linked Hybrid multi-functional urban block in Beijing (2003–2008), with more than 2,500 inhabitants; and the World Trade Center competition entry in New York (2002).[1] In the recent projects, the architect's interest has included serious applications of ecological solutions, such as geothermal heating and cooling and the recycling of water. The tireless sense of curiosity and mental energy that the majority of Holl's projects exude assure me that his expedition will also lead him into hitherto unexplored territories in the future.

Already during the early 1980s I had paid attention to the few of Steven Holl's published projects, such as the highly strategic Manila Housing Competition scheme (1975); the semi-underwater Sokol Retreat, St. Tropez (1976); the Bronx Gymnasium Bridge, New York (1977); the Bridge of Houses on Elevated Rail, New York (1980–82); and the Autonomous Artisans' Housing project, Staten Island (1980–84). I was intrigued by the combined ultra-rationality and surreal or dreamlike air of these architectural propositions as well as by the poetic precision of Holl's minimal line drawings, akin to the contemporaneous elegantly spare drawings of Mark Mack. The sense of life evoked by furniture and everyday objects made me think of the reduced perspective drawings of Heinrich Tessenow, which exude a warm feeling of lived domestic life. During the eighties I had also seen photographs of a couple of Holl's executed buildings in architectural journals: the Pool House and Sculpture Studio (Scarsdale, New York, 1980); the House at Martha's Vineyard (Massachusetts, 1984–88); and the Hybrid Building (Seaside, Florida, 1984–88), which all conveyed a similarly personal and focused architectural intention.

Holl's winning competition entry for the Amerika-Gedenkbibliothek (America Memorial Library, 1988) in Berlin—with its unorthodox volumetric composition and strangely swelling bridge element—suggested an urban architecture beyond both the modernist and postmodern imageries of the time. The interior perspectives of the project, with several stepped floors rising and receding in space, made me think of the endless maze of spaces and stairways in Giovanni Battista Piranesi's hypnotic *Carceri* etchings (1745–50). I also remember having recalled that when I saw the first published photographs of the Gothic towers of Louis Kahn's Richards Medical Research Building (1957–60) in Philadelphia in the early 1960s I had felt a similar sensation of dizziness as I realized that I was gazing at a new architectural world, the doors of which had just been opened.

Holl's inspired and meticulous studies of *American Vernacular Typologies* (1982) as well as his writings published since the late 1970s in the *Pamphlet Architecture* publications, which he himself edited, finally convinced me that here was an architect who seriously aspired to ground his work in

The Nelson-Atkins Museum of Art
Kansas City, MO, United States
1999–2007

The Nelson-Atkins Museum of Art
Kansas City, MO, United States
1999–2007

the mental and historical deep structures of architecture, and consequently, that he would very likely be capable of expanding the realm of contemporary architecture that seemed to be caught between a mannerist modernism and painfully eclectic postmodernist imageries.

My first live encounter with Steven Holl's designs took place at the exhibition of his work at the Museum of Modern Art in New York in 1989.[2] Particularly the elegant material constructions in the exhibition—made of blackened steel and bronze and frosted glass—appeared fresh and suggested to me a sensuous architecture that addresses imagination and the sense of touch. These constructions even seemed to sensitize other sensory modalities, and I realized that my own existential sense, my very sense of self, was being addressed and activated. Holl's exhibition architecture made me think of his slightly earlier New York projects: the Cohen Apartment (1982–83); the Kurtz Apartment (1985); the Pace Collection Showroom (1986); and the Giada Shop (1987), which conveyed a feeling of the abstracted rhythmical and geometric space of De Stijl Neo-Plasticism combined with a unity of space, sensuous materiality, and haptic evocation. I felt that the architect had now identified fully his personal artistic realm and expression.

While visiting the exhibition, I did not have the slightest idea that Steven and I would ever meet—in fact, fairly soon for that matter—let alone become intimate friends and even occasional collaborators.

In August 1991, in the middle of the intense intellectual discussions of the fifth Alvar Aalto Symposium in Jyväskylä in Central Finland, I enticed Steven to visit the extraordinary Petäjävesi Church, forty kilometers away, built in 1764 by a local peasant master builder. On the way to the church, I told Steven that the primitive drawing of a cross-shaped floor plan for the church, which the local farmer congregation had submitted to the Royal Swedish Court (Finland was part of Sweden at that time) for approval, had been rejected and stamped "unacceptable." Due to the slow pace of communications at the time, however, the villagers had already managed to build the church by the time the rejection letter from Stockholm reached the village. The humble church is now a monument protected by UNESCO. The touchingly sincere log vaults, imitating Renaissance stone structures, sealed our friendship, I believe.

Holl had built rather small residential structures and shop interiors until 1992, when he was commissioned to execute the Kiasma Museum of Contemporary Art on a central site in Helsinki (1992–98) on the basis of his winning entry in the international competition, which drew the record number of five hundred twenty entries. Despite the unarguable authority provided by his competition victory, the design task was exceptionally demanding contextually, functionally, technically, and even politically. In addition to the usual architectural considerations, Holl had to acquaint himself with the larger-than-life figure of Marshall Mannerheim, whose equestrian statue, next to the museum, evoked a public controversy about the suitability of Holl's museum on its site, and almost managed to sink the project. The museum commission eventually took Holl's architectural practice to new professional complexities and requirements.

Simultaneously with the Kiasma project, Holl and his office were working on two others that were equally challenging: the Cranbrook Institute of Science in Bloomfield Hills, Michigan (1993–98), the extension and renovation of the museum designed by Eliel Saarinen in 1931 (coincidentally, Kiasma is located only a block away from Eliel Saarinen's great Helsinki Railway Station); and the Chapel of St. Ignatius in Seattle (1994–97), the city of Holl's childhood and youth. These three projects established Steven Holl's position as one of the most innovative and prolific architects of our time. In them he developed his characteristic sensibilities for integral spaces that transcend the idea of additive assembly and for his characteristic strategies of reflected light and color, sensuous materiality, and haptic detailing. He also perfected his personal design methodology as well as his methods of collaborating with numerous assistants and expert consultants. His practice grew quickly into an international operation with numerous successful competitions and commissions in several European countries, the Near East, Japan, China, Korea, and Cambodia in addition to various cities in the United States.

Holl has always disliked the idea of a rationalized and instrumentalized practice; "corporate architecture" is a notion with heavily negative connotations in his language. Instead of using linear, repetitiously modular, and additive ideas, he has sought architectural singularities, and his buildings frequently appear as if they were carved or cast rather than assembled structures. These properties give rise to an experience of finiteness and uniqueness both in the ensemble and its parts. His surface

Sarphatistraat Offices
Amsterdam, The Netherlands
1996–2000

Sarphatistraat Offices
Amsterdam, The Netherlands
1996–2000

patterns, such as window and wall subdivisions, or even the composition of a set of cupboard doors and drawers, usually form interlocking figures that give rise to a visual coherence akin to the visual singularity of Eduardo Chillida's sculpture pieces. Holl's use of the golden section as his proportional system also strengthens this sense of coherence. "Proportion can be felt more than directly perceived," he points out. "It is, like cacophony and harmony in music, quite subjective and quite powerful."[3]

Holl's determined and continued experimentation and deliberate avoidance of a fixed signature style are made possible by his working method. He combines a subtle, artistically tuned, intimate and personal search through small watercolor sketches with the use of poetic verbal metaphors and potent conceptual diagrams (often drawn from scientific notions), studies in physical models and, finally, computer-generated development and production drawings. The computer is used for the purposes of developing the scheme and producing precise documents for execution, not for generating a formal language or expression. As Holl explains:

> We use computerized techniques in almost every stage of the design process except the initial conception. For me the original concept sketch must start with an analogue process intimately connecting mind-hand-eye. I feel this is the only way to be completely connected to the subtleties and qualities of the role intuition plays in conception. In the initial drawing, I feel a direct connection to spiritual meaning and the fusion of idea and space conception. After that the work can be digitally supercharged. The process can take off using all the rapid computerized tools possible.... In a positive sense, new computer potential has liberated our design process to be even more imaginative.[4]

The physical and mental intimacy and tactility of the early phases of work, combined with the architect's phenomenological interest in light, materiality, and detailing, secure the presence of the human hand in the encounter with the completed building. Holl's buildings usually project an intentional roughness instead of the usual slick perfection of today's avant-garde and minimalist architectures. This deliberate avoidance of the forced perfection of surfaces and finishes generates a sense of openness and presents an invitation instead of the air of exclusion and rejection often projected by buildings of obsessive technical perfection.

Steven Holl has managed to develop an exceptionally convincing interplay of thought and form, thinking and making, words and materials, technology and artistic expression. Architects' verbal philosophical formulations frequently contradict the characteristics of their design work, but Holl's physical forms and written words are cast of the same emotion and matter and are both based on the integration of perception, thought, and feeling. They do not arise from theoretical speculation and reason but from imagination and lived experience. In his first book, *Anchoring* (1989), Holl acknowledges these essential dialectics of design albeit with an air of hesitation:

> Writing's relation to architecture affords only an uncertain mirror to be held up to evidence; it is rather in a wordless silence that we have the best chance to stumble into that zone comprised of space, light, and matter that is architecture. Although they fall short of architectural evidence, words present a promise. The work is forced to carry over when words themselves cannot. Words are arrows pointing in the right directions; taken together, they form a map of architectural intentions.[5]

A decade or so later Holl already saw the role of philosophical investigation quite clearly and firmly:

> A philosophy of architecture, however casual, drives the work of any thinking architect. It has been an ongoing lifelong project for me to develop—parallel to built works—a written account of the aspiration of architecture as a form of thought. From my first little manifesto, *Anchoring* (1989), to our collaborative work, *Questions of Perception* (1994), a philosophy of architecture is the elusive but never achieved aim. The joy of building constructions driven by larger ideas is a wonderful mystery.[6]

Early on Holl began using verbal and literary concepts as energizing and guiding mental images in his design process. The Berkovitz House at Martha's Vineyard in Massachusetts (1984), for instance, was

Stretto House
Dallas, TX, United States
1989–91

Stretto House
Dallas, TX, United States
1989–91

inspired by Herman Melville's *Moby Dick,* or more precisely, by the story in the novel according to which the Indian tribe that originally inhabited this region created a unique dwelling type by stretching skins or bark over a whale skeleton that they found on the beach. Holl's house on the beach is a metaphorical skeleton, with the dense wooden frame standing for the whale's rib bones.

Holl named the various residential units of the Bridge of Houses project to suggest individualized dwellers and architectural narratives tailored for the personalized occupants: House of the Decider, House of the Doubter, House for a Man without Opinions, The Riddle, Dream House, Four Tower House, Matter and Memory. The fictitious clients that he imagined for his project for the Autonomous Artisans' Housing were: papermaker, woodworker, boatbuilder, mason, glass etcher, plasterer, and metalworker. Similarly, the imagined clients, "the society of strangers" of the Hybrid Building built in Florida, were: tragic poet, musician, and mathematician. The personification of dwellers in a housing project evidently helps Holl bridge the alienating void of anonymity; a profound architect envisions the life that takes place in the space he is designing, not solely its geometric and visual properties. "Let us assume a wall: what takes place behind it?" the poet Jean Tardieu advises us architects.[7] Yet we usually do not have the interest to imagine the lives that take place in the houses that we are designing.

Holl's project for the Knut Hamsun Center (1994–2009), currently in its final phase in Hamarøy, Norway, is a scheme driven by literary concepts from Hamsun's literary masterpiece *Hunger* (1890). The basic concept of a "body of invisible forces" is drawn from the writer's semi-delirious confession: "I was nothing but a battleground for invisible forces."[8] The architect has included other scenes from the novel, such as that of "a girl with her sleeves rolled up [who] leaned out and began polishing the panes on the outside."[9]

Holl has also used musical metaphors or analogues in his architectural work. The Stretto House in Dallas, Texas (1989–91) is based on the musical concept of "stretto" (a fugue motif used to accompany itself to form a counterpoint) and Bela Bartok's *Music for Strings, Percussion, and Celeste* (1937). The four movements of the musical score as well as its subdivision into percussion (heavy) and string (light) components are reflected in the spatial, formal, and material structures of the house. Another example of musical inspiration in Holl's work is the project for the Sarphatistraat Offices in Amsterdam (1996–2000), the reflected light and color of which, trapped behind the perforated metal façades, echo a concept deriving from the music of Morton Feldman's *Patterns in a Chromatic Field* (1981).

Steven Holl's most efficient creative tool is the concept—a potent fusion of a metaphor and an architectural idea in a singular guiding image. His metaphoric design concepts, such as Seven Bottles of Light in a Stone Box (Chapel of St. Ignatius); Strange Attractors, House of Vapor, Story of Water, Garden of Science, and House of Ice (an addition to the Cranbrook Institute of Science); Tripleness and Right Hand Rule (Bellevue Art Museum, 1997–2001), Menger Sponge (Sarphatistraat Offices), Porosity (Simmons Hall, 1999–2002), Stone and Feather (Nelson Atkins Museum, 1999–2007), and Writing with Light (Long Island, 2001–04), all suggest poetic or scientific images. Maurice Merleau-Ponty's notion of "chiasm," which the architect used as the guiding concept and code name of his competition entry for the Helsinki Museum of Contemporary Art, was later accepted as the very name of the museum, Kiasma.[10]

Beginning with his early career, Holl has been working with the strategy of "limited concept," which, as he writes, "is reformulated for each site and each unique program. . . . Language becomes the vehicle of 'recognition of the concept' as argued extensively by Ernst Cassirer in his book *Philosophy of Symbolic Forms* [1923–29]."[11] Holl explains the seminal role of conceptual diagrams in his design process, stating:

I depend entirely on concept diagrams, I consider them my secret weapon. They allow me to move afresh from one project to the next, from one site to the next. If I approached projects with a fixed vocabulary, I would be exhausted by now: I would have lost my interest in architecture long ago. Finding an initial concept for each project that captures the essence of architectural opportunities unique to that project is, for me, a way into it, the door through which new ideas enter architecture. Though many if not most people who appreciate my work seem to focus on its experiential or phenomenological qualities, the light, the use of materials, and so forth—for me, what is important is the idea.[12]

Kiasma Museum of Contemporary Art
Helsinki, Finland
1992–98

Kiasma Museum of Contemporary Art
Helsinki, Finland
1992–98

Holl valorizes his working method further in the conversation we had for the Spanish journal *El Croquis* in 2002, stating:

> A concept is the "engine" that drives the design process. Early in each project, after analyzing the site and program and sometimes after several false starts, a central concept (or concepts) [is] settled on, together with vague spatial sketches. As each site circumstance is unique, we aim for equally balanced and particular solutions. The concept, expressed in the diagram and words, helps focus a manifold of different aspects. It helps in the development of a project and communication with a client . . . In a sense the individual "poetic notations" are not just engines driving the design—they are great liberators connecting to broader thinking in other disciples.[13]

Holl's exceptional open-mindedness and receptiveness in his design process is exemplified by the sessions of critical conversations on projects under development in his office, often involving invited outside critics in addition to his office staff. During the design and development phases of the Kiasma project in Helsinki, I was often surprised by his willingness and capacity to accept suggestions or requirements from the client even though they sometimes seemed to be unreasonable and in conflict with the architect's initial aspirations. He was able to turn these incidents into positive impulses in the development process instead of regarding them as undesirable disturbances or compromises.

Regardless of his engagement in a conceptually driven design process, Steven Holl is one of the foremost representatives of the phenomenological approach in architecture today. Since his early writings and designs he has focused on the experiential and phenomenal dimensions of architecture that arise in the actual encounter with the work. Instead of the formalist concerns popular in today's architectural thinking, he explores the perceptual phenomena implicit in various aspects of the project and aims at mediating true sensory and mental experiences, particularly tactile qualities, "the haptic realm." His initial exploratory phase with watercolor sketches and the later development with physical models strengthen the presence of the material and experiential reality. Holl explains the phenomenological ground of his work:

> Architecture intertwines the perception of time, space, light, and materials, existing on a "pre-theoretical ground." The phenomena which occur within the space of a room, like the sunlight entering through a window, or the color and reflection of materials on a surface, all have integral relations in the realm of perception. The transparency of a membrane, the chalky dullness of plaster, the glossy reflection of opaque glass, and the beam of sunlight intermesh in reciprocal relationships that form the particular experience of a place.[14]

Considering Steven Holl's engagement in painting since his early youth, his collaborations with artists, and his passionate interest in the arts, it is hardly surprising that he has become one of the most trusted architects in the design of contemporary museums.[15] His list of projects currently includes more than a dozen competition entries and completed buildings for art museums and other art exhibition spaces. In addition, he has worked on nearly ten other museum projects, including museums for cinema and toys, natural history, human evolution, architecture, and Mediterranean civilizations.

The most recent of Holl's museum designs, the HEART Herning Museum of Contemporary Art, is an unconstrained and assured project by an experienced designer of spaces for art. As the site is opposite a former shirt factory (in which the museum temporarily operated), designed in the shape of a shirt collar, Holl continues the playful Oldenburgian Pop-Art imagery by conceiving the new museum in the image of shirtsleeves crossing each other. The two exhibition spaces proper, "the treasure boxes," are rationally rectangular spaces, whereas the building's other functions and facilities are grouped around this rectangular and functionally independent core, following a freely shaped contour. The architect himself emphasizes his intention to design the museum as a series of spatial experiences projected by the interplay of the *parti* of the museum and the adjacent earth berms instead of presenting the museum as an object.

The sectional strategy creates a lively rhythm of suspended sail forms, or diagonal wave patterns, across and independently of the plan configuration, providing varying daylight conditions in the exhibition spaces.

Not having visited the HEART, I must refrain from further describing the spaces and their characteristics, as the qualities of any profound architectural work that deliberately aims at the real physical encounter can only be experienced and judged in "the flesh of the world," to use a seminal notion of one of Holl's favorite philosophers, Merleau-Ponty.[16]

Whereas the construction of the HEART has taken place, another of Steven Holl's projects in the Nordic countries, the Knut Hamsun Center in Hamarøy, near the writer's birth place, far above the Arctic Circle in Norway, is currently in the final stages of construction after fifteen years of hesitation. This project, centering on the politically controversial literary figure, who won the Nobel Prize in 1920, reveals Holl's imaginative and empathetic capacities. The project merges a sense of Norwegian vernacular with surreal and uneasy imagery fully appropriate for the task. But this dreamlike air also seems to reconnect the architect back to the somewhat surreal ambience of his earliest projects. Through slight shifts and distortions (an unnoticeably inclined, apparently unstable tower with "hair" growing on its roof), Holl evokes a sense of the mystical and extraordinary that arises from images that simultaneously appear fairytale-like and familiar. The black tower arises simultaneously comfortably and disturbingly in the midst of traditional red-painted houses of northern Norway with their characteristic turf roofs, while the tower-shape also engages in a dialogue with the surrounding mountains. The building is related to its specific northern location by windows at the top, which permit the highest sun angle of forty-seven degrees to penetrate through the entire tower all the way to ground level. Holl's project demonstrates that architecture can narrate stories and that it has the power to poeticize facts of life, project significance on apparent meaninglessness, and reveal the mysteries behind our everyday experiences.

As Holl himself puts it: "We . . . are concerned with exploring the essential experiences of day-to-day phenomena. Ordinary and extraordinary facts, circumstances, and experiences, when seen as important, can generate a meaningful architecture."[17]

Notes

1   The project was produced in collaboration with Richard Meier and Partners, Eisenman Architects, and Gwathmey Siegel & Associates Architects.
2   Steven Holl / Emilio Ambasz exhibition, Museum of Modern Art, New York, February to April 1989.
3   Steven Holl and Juhani Pallasmaa, "A Conversation with Steven Holl: Thought, Matter and Experience," *El Croquis* 108 (2002), p. 24.
4   Ibid., p. 25.
5   Steven Holl, *Anchoring* (New York, 1989), p. 9.
6   Holl and Pallasmaa 2002, p. 12 (see note 3). Holl refers here to Steven Holl, Juhani Pallasmaa, and Alberto Pérez-Gómez, *Questions of Perception: Phenomenology of Architecture,* A + U Special Issue (July 1994).
7   As quoted in Georges Perec, *Tiloja avaruuksia* [Espèces d'espaces] (Helsinki, 1992), p. 72.
8   Knut Hamsun, *Hunger* (London, 1974), p. 15.
9   Hamsun 1974 (see note 8).
10 Merleau-Ponty describes the notions of intertwining and chiasm in his essay "The Intertwining—The Chiasm," in Maurice Merleau-Ponty, *The Visible and the Invisible,* ed. Claude Lefort, trans. Alphonso Lingis (Evanston, Illinois, 4th printing, 1992), pp. 130-55.
11 Holl and Pallasmaa 2002, p. 12 (see note 3).
12 As quoted in Yehuda E. Safran, "Steven Holl: Idea and Method," in *Steven Holl: Idea and Phenomena*, eds. Kerstin Gust, Isabella Marte, and Aislinn Weidele, (Baden, 2002), p. 73.
13 Holl and Pallasmaa 2002, p. 16 (see note 3).
14 Steven Holl, *Arc en rêve centre d'architecture* (Zurich, 1994), p. 3.
15 Holl's brother is a painter, and Steven himself began making paintings in 1959 before he became interested in architecture. Already at the age of twelve he exhibited his paintings at the Kitsap Country Fair in the State of Washington. Holl confesses that his encounters with Donald Judd, Dennis Oppenheim, Richard Nonas, Meg Webster, James Turrell, and other artists in New York after 1976 were seminal for the development of his architectural ideas. Holl and Pallasmaa 2002, p. 8 (see note 3). In his various projects Holl has collaborated with major artists such as Vito Acconci and Walter de Maria.
16 Merleau-Ponty describes the notion of "the flesh" in Merleau-Ponty 1992 (see note 10).
17 Steven Holl, Foreword to *Intertwining* (New York, 1996), p. 7.

Paul Gadegaard
Tabletop, 1960 / HEART

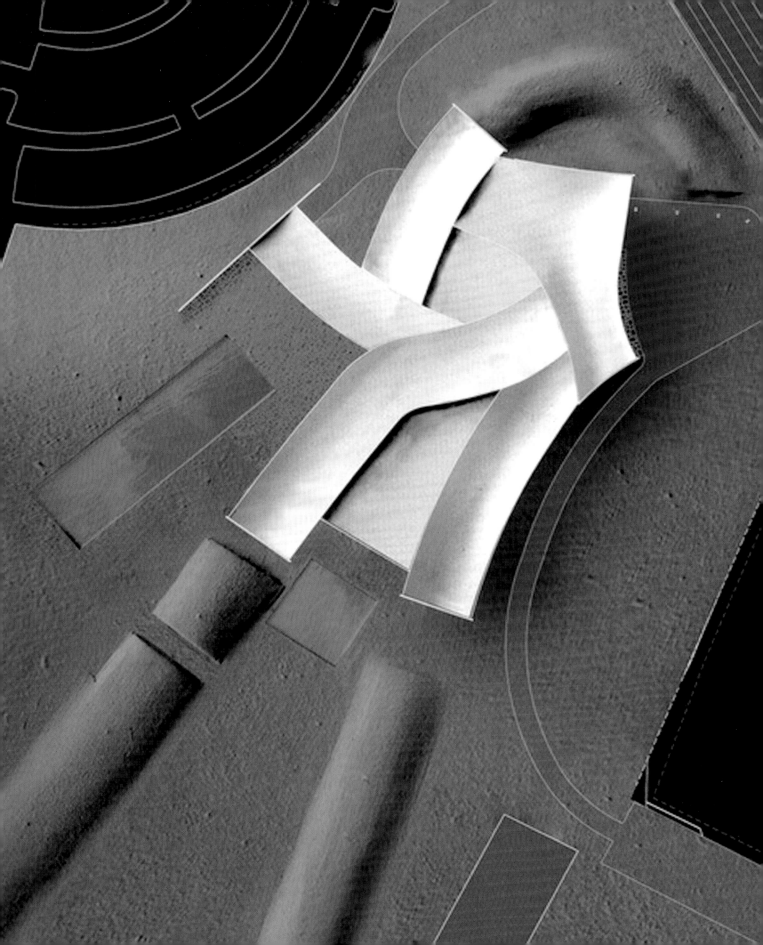

heart

Holger Reenberg

Konkurrencen 1

Da jeg første gang i foråret 2005 kom ind i det rum på Herning Kunstmuseum, hvori de anonymt indsendte plancher med arkitekturforslag hang, var der et, jeg ikke kunne få øjnene fra. Rummet, kaldet Stensalen, skulle i de kommende måneder huse den 13 mand store bedømmelseskomite, som skulle vælge det rigtige forslag til et nyt Herning Kunstmuseum.Det forslag, som særligt tiltvang sig min opmærksomhed, var i sort/hvid og helt åbenbart lavet i hånden! Med det mener jeg, at billederne af bygningen ikke var en tredimensionel computer visualisering, men en rigtig model.Planchernes billeder skiftede mellem modelfotos, håndtegninger og akvareller. Ja, med en smule selvironi kan man måske påstå, at det var kunsthistorikerens drøm af en præsentation, men desuden fremkaldte plancherne en række formelle og stoflige associationer til stedet, historien og kunsten.

Damgaard, Gadegaard og Manzoni

Herning Kunstmuseum havde siden indvielsen i 1977 haft til huse i Anglibygningen, Aage Damgaards skjortefabrik. Forinden havde Damgaard-familiens Midtjysk Skole- og Kulturfond overdraget de bedste dele af Aage Damgaards enestående kunstsamling til staten med henblik på oprettelsen af et statsanerkendt museum. Aage Damgaard havde således produceret skjorter i de lokaler, der kom til at huse Herning Kunstmuseum. På skjortefabrikken skabte han den model for samarbejde mellem erhvervsliv og kunstnere som var og er ganske unik i dansk sammenhæng.

Samarbejderne er også det historiske og idémæssige grundlag for Socle du Monde Biennalen, som åbnede første gang i 2002 og drives fra HEART i samarbejde med Erhvervsrådet.

I et brev fra sommeren 1960 på Missionshotellets brevpapir skriver Piero Manzoni hjem til en ven, at han er blevet ansat på Anglifabrikken og har fået en assistent med bil. Aage Damgaard var blevet gjort opmærksom på Manzoni af maleren Paul Gadegaard. Gadegaard selv var på det tidspunkt i fuld gang med udsmykningen af Damgaards nye fabriksbygning, kaldet Den Sorte Fabrik. Bygningens facade var ganske rigtig kulsort, men inden i var gulve, vægge, lofter malet i rene farver i abstrakte former. Paul Gadegaard havde fået frie hænder til at skabe en totaludsmykning af et hidtil uset omfang. Man kan godt påstå, at en hel generations drøm om at lade kunsten indtage det sociale rum kulminerede i Gadegaards arbejde i Herning i perioden 1952-82.

Manzoni gentog sit besøg i Herning den følgende sommer, igen med den samme frihed til helt at forfølge de kunstneriske mål, han måtte ønske. Af denne grund ejer Herning Kunstmuseum i dag 37 værker af Piero Manzoni bl.a. *La Linea Lunga* og *Socle du Monde*.

Der findes to helt afgørende omdrejningspunkter for driften af Herning Kunstmuseum. Det ene er samlingen af Piero Manzoni-værker: den største offentlige samling af Manzoni i verden, som året igennem udløser låneanmodninger fra museer kloden rundt. Det andet omdrejningspunkt er hele den permanente samlings afsæt i fabrikant Aage Damgaards private samling, og den unikke måde denne samling blev grundlagt på.I de seneste syv år har museet forsøgt at operationalisere disse to omdrejningspunkter ved at synliggøre dels Manzoni samlingen dels Aage Damgaards særlige mæcenvirksomhed i forbindelse med alle arrangementer og udstillinger.

Når det drejede sig om udlån af Manzonis værker, havde museet aldrig været i stand til at arrangere udstillinger baseret på modlån. Det skyldtes overvejende, at den gamle fabriksbygning var uegnet som udstillingssted. Museet havde altså ikke kunnet arrangere udstillinger, som befandt sig på samme niveau, som den samling, man var ejer af. I forbind-else med udlån af Manzoni til Guggenheim Museum i New York, måtte man bl.a. afslå tilbud om udlån af Guggenheims samling af Wassily Kandinsky værker.

Konkurrencen 2

Det var denne historie og kunsthistorie om Damgaard, Gadegaard og Manzoni, som de sort /hvide plancher i Stensalen umiddelbart og på uhåndgribelig vis syntes at fremmane. Forslagets umiskendelige fokus på det, kunstmuseet Louisianas grundlægger Knud W. Jensen kaldte "Stedets ånd", var ikke opnået gennem en fiks arkitektonisk metafor eller en direkte symbolsk form, selvom både symbolik og metaforik også var væsentlige elementer i helheden. Bygningen syntes så at sige at fremmane sig selv som en naturlig forlængelse af de konkrete omgivelser. Samtidig kombinerede den en klar funktionalitet i forhold til udstillingskravene med en poetisk forståelse af den kunst, den skulle huse. Hvad jeg ikke vidste dengang, men måske burde have kunnet gætte var, at arkitekten hed Steven Holl.

Jeg havde et vist kendskab til Steven Holls arkitektur fra min tid på Arken Museum for Moderne Kunst i København. Her var jeg ofte i dialog med Tuula Arkio og Maretta Jauku-uri henholdsvis direktør og chefkurator på Helsinkis museum for samtidskunst, KIASMA, som Holl var arkitekt på. Jeg hørte om samarbejdet og var også oppe for at se, hvordan byg-geriet skred frem. Et byggeri som kombinerede stor funktion-alitet og respekt for kunsten med et udtryksfuldt arkitekton-isk sprog. I Herning dukkede hans navn frem igen under Lars Damgaards og mine samtaler.

Konkurrencen blev udskrevet den 16. februar 2005. Man var enige om, at 6 tegnestuer kunne deltage, de fire gennem prækvalifikation og de to sidste skulle inviteres. Deltager-feltet kom til at bestå af CUBO og 3XNielsen – begge Århus – Snöhetta, Oslo, Keith Williams Architects, London, mens Steven Holl Architects, New York og Caruso St. John, London begge havde modtaget en særlig invitation. Det var en ganske fantastisk fornemmelse at være nået så langt, at man kunne påbegynde en konkurrenceperiode (30.5-9.9.2005) med del-tagelse af så stærke tegnestuer. Ikke mindst var det utro-ligt, at det var lykkedes at få Fonden Realdania interesseret i vores projekt . . . På det tidspunkt havde jeg været leder af Herning Kunstmuseum i fire år med den helt overgribende opgave at forsøge at realisere en ny museumsbygning.

2001-2005

I 2000 fik jeg en henvendelse fra Herning Kunstmuseums nye bestyrelsesformand, Lars Damgaard, Aage Damgaards søn, som også var direktør for A Hereford Beefstouw, som faren havde grundlagt. Det blev til et hurtigt møde, og Lars Dam-gaards ønske var utvetydigt: Herning Kunstmuseum skulle genstartes, og man skulle have en ny bygning! Der fulgte hur-tigt et par ansættelsessamtaler med bestyrelsen og i marts 2001 kunne jeg påbegynde mit nye job i Herning. Hvis et byg-geri som Steven Holls skal realiseres i en provinsby, kræver

det at momentet er rigtigt. Nu kan man med en lille smule lokal patriotisme spørge, om det ikke altid er sådan i Her-ning? Ganske vist er Herning kendt for sin driftighed, sit ini-tiativ og ikke mindst for evnen til samarbejde på tværs af politiske- og faggrænser for at nå store mål. Mål som ellers ofte er udenfor en dansk provinsbys rækkevidde. Alligevel krævedes der noget særligt denne gang. To gange tidligere havde museet forsøgt at realisere et nyt byggeri uden held.

Inden min ankomst havde projektet allerede fået et godt afsæt. Herning firmaet Wilton Tæppers nu afdøde grundlæg-ger og leder Johannes Jensen havde foræret Herning Kom-mune en grund med den forudsætning, at den skulle an-vendes til et nyt kunstmuseum. Museets bestyrelse var desuden sammensat af delvis nye medlemmer.

Lars Damgaard, folketings- og byrådsmedlemmet Johan-nes Poulsen og jeg indledte fra begyndelsen et frugtbart og tæt samarbejde. I 2002 blev Lars Krarup ny borgmester i Herning og hans engagerede holdning fik lige fra begyn-delsen afgørende betydning for projektets gennemførelse.

2002 blev det år hvor en række indledende kontakter og beslutninger blev taget. Det blev året, som kom til at afstikke den kurs, som skulle vise sig at være den rigtige. Herning Kunstmuseum indledte sammen med Erhvervsrådet bien-nalen Socle du Monde. En biennale hvis udgangspunkt var samarbejdet mellem kunstnere og erhvervsliv, vel at mærke helt i Aage Damgaards ånd, med fuld kunstnerisk frihed. Næsten samtidig enedes Herning Kommune og museet om, at lade det nyligt etablerede landsdelsensemble Ensemble MidtVest få residency i et eventuelt nyt museum.

Vi tog også den første kontakt til Henning Kruse Petersen, daværende koncerndirektør for kreditinstituttet Nykredit. Kruse Petersen skulle senere blive formand for det præsi-dium, hvis opgave det var at rejse penge til byggeriet. Kruse Petersen tilførte hele processen sit store netværk og en ny dynamik. Vigtigst af alt, fik vi de første møder med Fonden Realdania, som viste interesse og besluttede at bekoste en undersøgelse ved PLS Rambøll, der skulle vurdere projek-tets bæredygtighed. Rambøll leverede sin positive rapport i begyndelsen af 2004. Rapporten konkluderede bl.a., at den væsentligste forudsætning for projektets succes var Herning Kunstmuseums Manzoni-samling. På baggrund af rapporten besluttede Realdania at bevilge midler til afholdelse af en arkitektkonkurrence.

HEART

Der findes arkitektur, som gør sig godt på en skærm eller et lærred, men som aldrig burde finde vej til en byggeplads i den virkelige verden, og der findes arkitektur som er tegnet af mennesker til mennesket og verden. Der er i løbet af de seneste 20 år blevet bygget mange nye kunstmuseer, hvis arkitektur i sig selv kan være interessant, men også er komplet uegnede som kunstmuseer eller blot udstillingssteder. Ja, det vil sige det kommer selvfølgelig an på hvilket museum man ønsker sig, hvilken rolle det skal spille, og hvordan man ønsker kunsten præsenteret.

Når man hører kuratorer og museumsdirektører tale om "den hvide kube", det anonyme, fleksible, firkantede rum som den eneste ideelle løsning på udstillingsrummet, så synes man også at fornemme et ønske om, at museumsarkitekturen ikke bør udvikle eller ændre sig. Kravet om et anonymt udstillingsrum knytter sig dels til forestillingen om kunsten som autonom, dels et ønske om fleksibilitet, således at rummet kan indrettes til at præsentere værket optimalt. Udtrykket "Det autonome kunstværk" dækker over en opfattelse af kunstens kvalitet som stående over og uden for stort set alt andet. Mesterværket kan så at sige forstås som netop mesterværk helt uafhængig af alle ydre faktorer. Det er naturligvis ikke rigtigt, i hvert tilfælde ikke helt!

Et hvilket som helst værk kan ikke forstås som kunst af hvem som helst. Den erkendelse er et væsentligt parameter for kunstmuseernes mulighed for at komme i dialog med publikum. Derfor! Hvis kunstværket i opfattelses- og erkendelsesprocessen er afhængigt af så mange faktorer, hvorfor så ikke af rummet? Og i så fald hvorfor altid af et hvidt anonymt rum, som i sin videste konsekvens ender som en form for global corporate identity.

Der er så vidt jeg kan se ikke tale om et enten eller i diskussionen af såvel det autonome kunstværk som udstillingsrummet. Der kan laves kunstmuseer i kirker, landsbyer, på øde strandbredder, i storcentre eller i bjergpas, og man kan udstille hvad man vil i dem. Man er på den ene side nødt til at erkende, at museets indre og ydre i dag er i en voldsom og modsætningsfyldt dialog med det omgivende samfund. Den udfordring må man tage op med de mange sociale fordele og de farer for kontaminering af museets kerne, det indebærer. På den anden side kan man også hævde, at en del af de værker, som finder vej til et museum, som er og bør forblive en historisk institution, har opnået en vis grad af selvstændigt liv, en form for indiskutabel status, i det mindste for en tid? I den tid og i det rum kan man så indimellem forsøgsvis isolere dem fra forbrugersamfundets og politikkens aktuelle dagsorden.

I konkurrence programmet kaldte vi det "det åbne skatkammer". Et hus som i sin periferi er åbent og opsøgende og sit indre indeholder rigtige skatkamre, som modspiller den ydre åbenhed. Det blev en lang og til tider vanskelig opgave for dommerkomiteen at finde den rigtige vinder, men den 14. oktober 2005 kunne man offentliggøre Steven Holls vinderprojekt, og den 25. juni 2007 kunne det første spadestik tages.

Da vinderprojektet var blevet offentliggjort skrev professor og landskabsarkitekt Steen Høyer i Arkitekten (1, 2006): "Det er i dag sjældent at se en talentfuld arkitekt, der tager sig selv og opgaven alvorligt, uden at lade show-off og kommercielle skovtursprogrammer præge projektet...Bygherren ønsker en alvor omkring kunstens udtryk. En fast og udtryksfuld ramme, som giver modspil uden at være en aggressiv eller smart modstander...De fleste af arkitekterne ser kunsten som et forbrugsgode, der kan indgå i det demokratiske landskab på almindelige markedsvilkår. Bygherren ønsker deri-

mod at fastholde værket og det unikke med en værdig bygning i Birk".

I hver sin ende af Birk Centerpark ligger der nu to afgørende forskellige strukturer med hver deres stærke skulpturelle kvaliteter. Det ene Ingvar Crohammars Elia, som blev indviet i 2001, er en mystikers værk, som uden årsag eller mål annullerer den hvide erhvervsparks nyttige stræben. Det andet er Steven Holls nye, og ja hvide museumsbygning med navnet HEART.

Navnet og den visuelle identitet med den karakteristiske skrifttype blev skabt af Kontrapunkt i 2007. Holls bygning er som alle hans bygninger skabt til sit "sted" og her med det formål at være museum. De associationer og referencer, som jeg instinktivt opfattede første gang jeg så konkurrenceplancherne blev i første omgang formidlet af facaderne med deres tilnærmede funktionelle geometri og tagkonstruktionens antropomorfe udtryksfuldhed. Forholdet mellem det organiske og geometriske parafraserer Paul Gadegaards konkrete kunst, som tilsyneladende tog udgangspunkt i det tiloversblevne stof fra skjorteproduktionen på Angli.

HEARTs tema er stofligt. Ydermurene er støbt på stedet i indfarvet hvid beton og facaderne møder os med en krøllet tekstilagtig overflade. Den stoflige reference føres videre i taget, som styrer grundplanen. Taget er sammensat af 5 skaller, som minder om skjorteærmer skåret igennem på langs. Ærmerne skaber stærke associationer til Utzon husets rejste skaller. Som sådan, med de lette krøllede mure og de hængende ærmer, virker HEART som et telt i beton. I tagets ærmestruktur er der indlagt to sænkede flade tage. Ærme og flade føjes sammen af et lodret bånd af sandslebet kanalglas, som forsyner udstillingsrummene med dagslys.

Grundplanens afgørende kerne er de to udstillingsrum, hvis vægges retvinklede linearitet modspiller loftets organiske karakter.

Grundplanens hovedgreb, hvorved udstillingsrummene er placeret som rektangulære/kvadratiske kuber på en "overdækket plads", omkranses af de øvrige funktioner, som alle er placeret i bygningens skal, opfylder konkurrenceprogrammets ønsker om en generel åbenhed kombineret med "skatkammer" ideen.

HEARTs sprog er ikke et autoritært arkitektursprog, som er sænket ned fra det ydre rum med henblik på at skabe et "andet sted", hvor økonomi, politik, livsstil er eller bliver de afgørende parametre. Tværtimod forholder museumsbygningens formgivning sig dels til sine nærmeste naboer, Utzons prøvehus og Anglifabrikken og dels til den historie, som har skabt stedet og den enstående kunstsamling, som huset i sidste ende skal rumme.

monochrome

Steven Holl

Nemchinova

Da det var vores første tur til Moskva, ville vi gerne besøge gravmælet over Kazimir Malevich, som vi havde set på fotografier; en hvid kube med et sort kvadrat. I vores email-udveksling med vores venner, arkitekterne og professor Vladimir og Ludmilla Kirpichev, bad vi dem om at medtage stedet i vores rejseplan. Ludmilla fortalte os så at gravmælet, såvel som det enorme egetræ, det stod under, blev ødelagt under anden verdenskrig. Hun skrev: "At tage til Nemchinova er at tage ingen steder hen …" Min kone, kunstneren Solange Fabião, svarede omgående: "… så må vi absolut tage derhen!"

Jeg havde været besat af Malevichs arbejde siden midten af 1970erne, hvor jeg opdagede hans malerier *White on White* (1918) og *Black Square* (1915) og hans suprematistiske manifest. Efter min ankomst til New York i 1977 var alle mine tegninger sort/hvide gennem fire år. Solange havde været besat af Malevich siden hendes år i Berlin på Akademie der Künste i 1986-88.

På en solrig morgen i marts sad vi så sammen i en lejet bil på vej fra Moskva til Nemchinova. Under den klare blå himmel så vi spredte områder af sne. Efter en flere timer lang køretur nåede vi frem til en spredt bebyggelse af relativt nybyggede dachaer (sommerhuse), og her fandt vi en gade, der hed "Malevich." Vi drejede ned af en sjappet vej og nåede kort efter frem til en lysning. Der stod en stor hvid kube med et rødt kvadrat. På den stod skrevet, "… her stod min faders grav, sådan som jeg husker den …" Den rekonstruerede kubus blev rejst af Malevichs datter i 1989, året før hun døde. Vladimir og Ludmilla så vantro til, og Solange og jeg var begejstrede for at opdage dette sted i Nemchinova. Senere fandt vi den grønne dacha af træ, som Malevich havde brugt om sommeren; den var markeret med en bronzeplade.

Monochromer, achromer, Malevich & Manzoni

Når man tænker på de 37 originale arbejder af Piero Manzoni i HEART Herning Museum of Contemporary Art, kan man ved at kigge tilbage se en åndelig bro, der forbinder Malevichs skrifter og optagethed af det monokrome med Piero Manzoni's achromer.

Holger Reenberg har skrevet om forbindelsen mellem Malevich og Manzoni, der ønskede "at nå det nulpunkt, hvorfra alt er muligt…" Selv om jeg var bekendt med Piero Manzonis arbejde, opdagede jeg først, at han havde skabt mange af sine vigtigste værker i Herning, da jeg læste det udvidede hæfte til konkurrencen for Hernings nye Kunstens Hus. Dette sted, midt i den jyske halvø, syntes at være ladet med den mystiske energi fra 1960ernes Arte Povera, fra Gruppo Zero og Malevichs monokromatiske ørkengrund.

Vi var blandt de i alt seks arkitekter, der blev inviteret til at deltage i konkurrencen om at skabe det nye kunstens hus i Herning; et sted, der skulle ligge tæt på den oprindelige skjortefabrik, som nu fungerer som museum. Grundplanen af denne bygning fra 1960erne havde samme facon som en skjortekrave … Herning var et interessant, idiosynkratisk sted. Selv om vi havde modtaget konkurrencebeskrivelsen og hæftet i april eller maj, havde vi så travlt med andet arbejde og andre konkurrencer, at vi var nødt til at udsætte arbejdet på Herning-konkurrencen. (Den sommer, i 2005, vandt vi tre konkurrencer i træk, heriblandt Knokke-Heist Hotel i Belgien og Cité du Surf i Biarritz). I slutningen af august læste jeg konkurrencebeskrivelsen igen og accepterede med stor entusiasme de fremsatte begrænsninger for bygningen, heriblandt maksimumhøjden på otte meter og påbuddet om at bruge farven hvid.

Jeg granskede Piero Manzonis værk nøje som én måde at finde ind i konkurrencen på. Hans *Socle du Monde* havde inspireret mig flere år forinden i forbindelse med mine studier af arbejder af Robert Smithson, Michael Heizer og andre konceptuelt orienterede kunstnere, der arbejder med landskabet. Piero Manzoni var gået forud for dem alle med *Socle du Monde*, der blev skabt i Herning. Mange stofeksperimenter i rækken af achromer var også blevet til på fabrikken i Herning. Som et bindeled til disse værker tegnede vi en bygning skabt i hvid beton, der er støbt in-situ, og hvor formene er foret, så der skabes linier der indfanger teksturen af krøllet stof.

Jeg fandt ved et tilfælde ud af, at min yndlingsarkitekt fra Danmark, Jørn Utzon, har bygget et af sine prototypehuse fra 1972 ved siden af museets grund. Huset er nu en smukt vedligeholdt privatbolig, og dens forhold til den nye bygning var vigtig for vores udgangspunkt.

Skattekister / skjorteærmer

Da der var lidt over en uge tilbage, tilbragte jeg en weekend med at lave skitser til et koncept. Jeg besluttede at lade udstillingsrummene fremstå som to "skattekister" eller æsker – som rektangler i centrum af grundplanen, hvorover kurvede, spredte tagelementer ville fange lyset. Det flade, ensartede landskab fik sit aftryk i den omvendte kurve i tagets geometri og fik dermed arkitektur og natur til at smelte sammen. Set fra luften mindede formerne om skjorteærmer, der er kastet hen over nogle æsker. Plantegningens løse kanter kunne tilpasses for at gøre plads til caféen, auditoriet og lobbyen, og de ortogonale, altså vinkelrette, udstillingsrum kunne aflukkes separat med henblik på brug af bygningen udover almindelig besøgstid. Idet hele bygningen er i ét plan, ville den have en glimrende luftcirkulation og være geotermisk opvarmet og nedkølet.

Med sin klare forankring i bygningens lokalområde forekom dette koncept velvalgt. Interiøret ville blive vakt til live af et gradueret, kurvet lys. Om mandagen kom jeg ind på tegnestuen med skitserne og spurgte tre assistenter, om de kunne lave præsentationen i løbet af den uge, der var tilbage inden deadlinens udløb. Efter deres entusiastiske "Ja!" måtte vi gennem adskillige nætters arbejde, inden vi nåede vores deadline – men de færdige præsentationsplancher med sort/hvide fotografier af den lille model så forrygende ud. Jeg forestillede mig et fantastisk lysindfald i de retvinklede udstillingsrum. I tidens diskussioner hører man ofte klicheerne om, hvordan nye kunstmuseer enten har så stærkt et udtryk, at de ikke egner sig som udstillingssted, eller også går til den anden yderlighed: en samling hvide kasser, der dræner kunsten for liv. Men vi tog en tredje vej. Hele præsentationen – alle syv plancher – holdt sig rent i sort og hvid.

Skandinavisk blod / nordisk lys

Min bedstefar blev født i Tønsberg, Norge. Min far, som var fuldblods nordmand, opfostrede os på kanten af Puget Sound, nær Seattle. Det lave, nordlige vinterlys har en særlig inspirerende kraft, der minder om det skandinaviske lys. I 1993 blev vi inviteret til at deltage i en konkurrence om at tegne et museum for samtidskunst i Helsinki. Konceptet, der fremlagde en sammensmeltning af det nordiske lys, byens stoflighed og landskabet i vores forslag, "Kiasma", viste sin styrke, da vores projekt blev valgt blandt de 516 forslag. En særlig opmærksomhed på det lavtstående sollys i Helsinki gav anledning til en sektion, der specifikt omhandlede hvordan lyset kunne indfanges.

Netop nu er vi i færd med at færdiggøre Knut Hamsun Centeret, der ligger over den arktiske cirkel i Hamarøy, Norge. Her er det nordiske lys særligt ekstremt – der er seks ugers midnatssol om sommeren og slet ingen sol i januar.

Disse byggeerfaringer og mit skandinaviske blod gav mig et forspring, når det gjaldt om at tænke en bygning, der

kunne udnytte det særlige, stedsspecifikke lys i Herning. De kurvede, "skjorteærmeagtige" tage vender opad og har striber af tagvinduer, der fanger den lavtstående sol og lader sollyset lige netop røre det nedadkurvede loft. Geometrien i de lysreflekterende kurver fordeler lyset så smukt i rummene, at de kan anvendes uden brug af kunstigt lys. Rummet bevæges og vækkes til live, når en sky bevæger sig hen over eller væk fra solen, sådan som det ofte sker i dette område.

Fladearkitektur / stoflige former

Fladerne i de kurvede tagelementer, der er draperet over udstillingsrummenes æskeformede skattekister blev efterfulgt af udviklingen af de øvrige rums flader, der er fremstillet i hvid beton. Der blev lagt presenninger i betonstøbningsformene for at skabe en stofagtig tekstur, der opsluger de små bump og buler, som en hurtig byggeproces medfører. Gulve af beton samler hele grundplanen med sin konsekvent gennemgående patina og voksfinish. Det slørede lys i f.eks. caféen blev opnået ved hjælp af sandblæst glas. Jordvolde fører bygningens geometri ind i landskabet og danner rum rundt om bygningen. Ved indgangen skaber de kurvede forhøjninger et rum, der beskytter bygningen mod den nærved liggende motorvej.

På sydsiden samler og reflekterer lange spejldamme sollyset over på udhængene. Landskabsarkitekten Torben Schønherr har udviklet videre på vores konkurrencekoncept med sine delikate, porøse belægninger og beplantninger.

Et telefonopkald ved Halloween

Efter at vi lige netop have nået vores deadline for at indsende plancherne vendte vi vores opmærksomhed mod andet arbejde og glemte alt om konkurrencen. Men den 31. oktober – altså dagen for Halloween – fik jeg et telefonopkald fra museumsdirektør Holger Reenberg, "Steven, du har vundet konkurrencen! Vi vil bygge dit hus og flytte ind inden for to år!" Idet telefonopkaldet kom fra København, kunne man ikke vide, hvilke implicitte betydninger det havde, at det ankom på dagen for Halloween; i New York er det en dag, der blander frygt og fryd.

Virkeliggørelsen: Et overraskende, luministisk rum

"Questions of Perception" ("Spørgsmål om Perception"), der blev skrevet sammen med Juhani Pallasmaa og Alberto Perez-Gomez i 1994, indeholder et kapitel med titlen "Perspective Space: Incomplete Perception" ("Det perspektiviske rum: Den ufuldendte perception"). Argumentet heri er at vores oplevelse – perception – af rum udvikles via en række overlappende perspektiver, der folder sig ud i overensstemmelse med den relevante vinkel, hastighed og bevægelse. Selv om vi kan analysere vores bevægelse langs en specifik rute ved en given hastighed, vil vi aldrig kunne redegøre for alle de synsvinkler, der er mulige.

Bygningen i Herning er en fysisk udmøntning af de tanker. Snarere end at være en bygning, der først opleves som et objekt, frembyder den en række udvendige oplevelser, der

Steven Holl Architects / Watercolor / HEART

smelter sammen med landskabet. Idet man bevæger sig rundt om bygningens eksteriør oplever man meget forskelligartede rum, der ikke tilsammen danner ét enkelt objekt, et enkeltstående hele. At træde ind i bygningen er en ganske anden oplevelse. Der er et element af overraskelse, især hvis man træder ind ved dagens afslutning, hvor den lavtstående sol i vest nærmest synes at eksplodere gennem de to lavt slyngende kurver, der fanger lyset i loftet.

Idet man bevæger sig fremad gennem de retlinede vægge, der omgiver udstillingslokalerne, glider rummet fra det ene til det andet, der hvor loftets skinnende kurve følger en strøm gennem flere på hinanden følgende rum. Udstillingsrummene, hvor væggene altid møder gulvet i en ret vinkel, er udformet således at der er fokus på kunsten, men i bygningens periferi bliver kanterne blødere og interagerer med landskabet. Caféen flyder over i terrasserne. Ensemble MidtVests koncertsal åbner sig ud imod sine egne øvelokaler og servicerum og knytter samtidig an til hovedlobbyen. Udstillingslokalerne i bygningens midte kan nemt aflukkes, samtidig med at alle rum i bygningens yderkanter forbliver åbne; f.eks. i forbindelse med arrangementer efter almindelig lukketid. Den monokrome ramme skaber særlig opmærksomhed om kunstens farver, der ændrer rummet alt efter den enkelte kunstners og udstillings særlige udtryk. Det retlinede udstillingsrum er blevet finpudset, så det er i overensstemmelse med forholdet 1:1.618 – lige som i alle vores andre projekter. I sin vigtige bog "The Geometry of Art and Life" fremfører Matila Ghyka et argument for at anvende proportioner, der er baseret på matematiske principper, der optræder i naturen; det gyldne snits forholdstal på 1:1.618 er et nøgletal for organisk vækst.

Når man vandrer gennem de rum, der forbinder administrationslokalerne, mærker man den energi, der skabes af lofternes kurvede flader – der her beskriver en opadgående kurve ud imod landskabet udenfor. For alle, der arbejder i museet, vil hverdagens opgaver blive livet op af arkitekturens fladeprægede og lysopsamlende geometri, der også knytter an til landskabet uden for. Museumsarkitekturens monokromatiske rammer bringes til live af ændringerne i lysindfaldet, både i løbet af en enkelt dag og med årstidernes skiften. Håbet er, at museet med sin koncertsal, der også kan fungere som auditorium, sit uddannelses- og formidlingscenter, sin restaurant og sine udendørs faciliteter kan fungere som et socialt samlingspunkt for lokalsamfundet. Museets kerne – udstillingsrummene – sigter efter at skabe et "luministisk" rum for skiftende kunstudstillinger.

Ved sit første møde med huset sagde kunstneren Jannis Kounellis at rummene minder ham om skure, hvorpå der hænger fiskenet. Måske kan man her indlæse lidt af havet i det flade midtjyske landskab. En forhøjning i landskabet, der bliver til bølger af lys, der markerer et "nulpunkt", som Piero Manzoni sagde …"hvor alt er muligt".

tanke og fænomen

Juhani Pallasmaa

"Den arkitektoniske tanke er en gennemarbejdning af fænomener, der opstår ud af ideer. Ved at 'skabe' indser vi, at ideer blot er et frø, der kan vokse videre i fænomenernes verden."
Steven Holl, *Anchoring*

Steven Holl har haft en lang og overraskende arkitektonisk løbebane, der tegner en kurve fra midt-70ernes tidlige projekter – der afspejlede stemningen fra samtidens italienske rationalisme – frem til det afslappede og oplevelsesmæssigt mangefacetterede HEART Herning Museum of Contemporary Art, der indvies i indeværende år. De femogtyve års kalendertid, der adskiller disse to poler i hans karrieres faser, synes at sammenfatte mere end én levealders intens kreativ udforskingsaktivitet inden for byggekunstens formelle, perceptuelle og mentale grundsten. Hans rejse som arkitekt har som pejlemærker haft en utrættelig læsning af digtekunsten (heriblandt værker af digtere som Osip Mandelstam, Anna Ahmatova og Paul Celan i tilgift til de digtere, hvis hovedsprog er engelsk), filosofien og den videnskabelige litteratur, såvel som et dybt engagement i den visuelle kunst. Spændvidden i hans designarbejde er imponerende varieret, men samtidig konsekvent, som havde det fulgt en nøje forudbestemt plan. Hans sti har slået folder og forgrenet sig i nye retninger, men samtidig har den også gradvist og på overbevisende vis skabt den enestående og let genkendelige verden, der tilhører netop arkitekten Steven Holl. At han for nylig fik tildelt den unikke *Frontiers of Knowledge Prize in the Arts,* sponsoreret af den spanske BBVA Bank, understreger det faktum, at han har opnået den højest tænkelige internationale anerkendelse for sin arkitektur. Der kan heller ikke være tvivl om, at han i løbet af de to seneste årtier også har været blandt de mest inspirerende forbilleder inden for arkitekturuddannelserne verden over. Hans åbenhed og nysgerrighed, såvel som hans sjældne evne til at sammenføje kreativt design med filosofisk klarhed og poetiske litterære udtryk, har forstærket hans indvirkning inden for arkitekturuddannelsen.

Kunstneres og arkitekters kunstneriske univers har det med at blive stadigt mere idiosynkratisk, snævert og hermetisk med tiden som en naturlig følge af en bevidst efterstræbelse efter en let genkendelig kunstnerisk identitet. Holls verden er blevet ved med at åbne sig for ny inspiration, nye ting at stræbe efter, nye arkitektoniske løsninger. Hans bygninger er ikke variationer over fasttømrede arkitektoniske anatomier, eller over hans egne tidligere arkitektoniske temaer; de er oftest nye arkitektoniske typologier, anatomier, og rumlige oplevelser. Hans tidlige interesse i arkitektoniske typologier har senere afspejlet sig i hans fortsatte stræben efter at skabe nye arkitektoniske typer; hvad man også kunne kalde nye arkitektonisk skabninger. Det synes som om han giver en indsprøjtning af ny arkitektonisk DNA i hver eneste ny opgave, og derved skaber han en ny og uforudset form for arkitektur hver gang. Tænk blot på de dramatiske forskelle mellem f.eks. det labyrintiske koncept for *Palazzo del Cinema* i Venedig (1990), der minder noget om menneskehjernens folder; på sammensætningen af formet og moduleret lys i

Chapel of St. Ignatius i Seattle (1994–97); den gigantiske, porøse, urbane væg og de konstruerede huler i kollegierne på *Simmons Hall* i Boston (1992–2002); den sølvagtige ekstruderede form på *Whitney Water Purification Facility* i Connecticut (1998–2005), der giver mindelser om vandets livgivende renhed, samt de oplyste lanterner eller "linser" af glasplanker i *Nelson-Atkins Museum of Art* in Kansas City (1999–2007), der rejser sig med stor autoritet fra jorden. Uanset hans interesse i integrerede rum og former skaber han ind imellem projekter, der er baseret på en strengt retvinklet geometri og et simpelt tektonisk sprog, f.eks. i *Swiss Residence* i Washington D.C. (2001–06), i *Writing With Light House*, Long Island (2001–04), og *Planar House*, Arizona (2002–05).

Som alle andre arkitekter begyndte Holl sin karriere med små teoretiske projekter, butiksinteriører, renoveringer, og huse, men han har i de senere år udført enorme urbane projekter såsom *Makuhari Housing*-projektet i Chiba, Japan (1992–96), den multifunktionelle karré *Linked Hybrid* i Beijing (2003–2008), der huser mere end 2.500 indbyggere, og et konkurrencebidrag til *World Trade Center*-konkurrencen i New York (2002)[1]. I Holl's senere projekter har arkitektens interesse blandt andet angået en seriøs brug af økologiske løsninger såsom geotermisk opvarmning og nedkøling samt genbrug af vand. Den utrættelige nysgerrighed og mentale energi, der strømmer fra Holls projekter, overbeviser mig om, at hans afsøgninger også fremover vil føre ham ind i uudforskede territorier.

Allerede i de tidlige 1980ere havde jeg bidt mærke i de få offentliggjorte projekter, der da fandtes fra Steven Holls hånd, såsom det meget strategiske koncept til *Manila Housing Competition* (1975); det særegne *Sokol Retreat*, St. Tropez, der ligger delvis under vandet (1976); *Bronx Gymnasium Bridge*, New York (1977); *Bridge of Houses on Elevated Rail*, New York (1980–82) samt projektet *Autonomous Artisans' Housing*, New York (1980–84). Min interesse blev vakt af kombinationen af det ultra-rationelle og det surrealistiske; det drømmeagtige skær, der kendetegnede disse arkitektoniske forslag, såvel som den poetiske præcision, der findes i hans minimalistiske stregtegninger, der bringer mindelser om de samtidige, elegant enkle tegninger af Mark Mack. Den følelse af liv, der vækkes af møblerne og hverdagsgenstandene mindede mig om det reducerede perspektiv i Heinrich Tessenows tegninger, der emmer af hjemmelivets varme. I løbet af 1980erne så jeg også fotografier af et par af Holls udførte bygninger i arkitekturmagasiner: hans *Pool House and Sculpture Studio* (Scarsdale, New York, 1980); hans *House at Martha's Vineyard* (Massachusetts, 1984–88), samt hans *Hybrid Building* (Seaside, Florida, 1984–88), der alle formidlede en tilsvarende personlig og fokuseret arkitektonisk hensigtserklæring.

Holls vinderforslag til arkitektkonkurrencen for *Amerika-Gedenkbibliothek* i Berlin (1988) antydede med den uortodokse volumenkonstruktion og det sært svulmende bro-element en urban arkitektur, der strakte sig hinsides tidens modernistiske og postmoderne formsprog. Projektets interiørperspektiver, hvori adskillige etager rejste sig i trapper og fortonede sig ud i rummet, fik mig til at tænke på den endeløse labyrint af rum og trapper i Piranesis hypnotiske *Carceri*-tegninger. Jeg husker også at være blevet mindet om dengang jeg i de tidlige 1960ere så de første offentliggjorte fotografier af de gotiske tårne på Louis Kahns *Richard's Medical Research Building* i Philadelphia; på det tidspunkt oplevede jeg en tilsvarende svimlende fornemmelse, da jeg blev klar over, at jeg betragtede en ny arkitektonisk verden, hvis døre netop var blevet åbnet.

Holls dybt beåndede og omhyggelige studier af værket *American Vernacular Typologies* (1982), såvel som hans eget forfatterskab, der siden slutningen af 1970erne blev udgivet I *Pamphlet Architecture*-rækken, som han selv redigerede, bibragte mig den endelige overbevisning om, at der her var tale om en arkitekt, der seriøst stræbte efter at forankre sit arbejde i arkitekturens dybe mentale og historiske strukturer; en arkitekt, der dermed havde gode chancer for at være i stand til at udvide den verden af samtidig arkitektur, der syntes fanget mellem en manieret modernisme og en ubehageligt eklektisk postmodernisme.

Mit førstehåndsmøde med Steven Holls arbejde fandt sted ved udstillingen af hans værker på Museum of Modern Art i New York in 1989[2]. Især udstillingens elegante konstruktioner af sort stål, bronze og sandblæst glas fremstod nyskabende og fremkaldte tanker om en sensuel arkitektur, der henvender sig til fantasien og følesansen. Konstruktionerne syntes også at øge finfølelsen hos andre sansemodaliteter, og jeg blev klar over at min egen eksistentielle sans, min fornemmelse for mit eget selv, var taget i tale og i færd med at blive aktiveret. Holls udstilling bragte mindelser om hans lidt tidligere projekter i New York: hans *Cohen Apartment* (1982–83); hans *Kurtz Apartment* (1985); *Pace Collection Showroom* (1986), samt *Giada Shop* (1987), der formidlede en fornemmelse for De Stijl neo-plasticismens abstrakte rytmiske og geometriske rum sammenføjet med en helstøbt fornemmelse for rum, en sanselig materialitet og noget haptisk stimulerende. Jeg følte, at arkitekten på det tidspunkt havde fundet sin helt personlige kunstneriske verden, sit helt eget udtryk.

Under mit besøg på udstillingen havde jeg ikke den ringeste idé om, at Steven og jeg nogensinde ville mødes – hvad vi rent faktisk gjorde relativt kort tid efter – og blive nære venner og ind imellem endog samarbejdspartnere.

I august 1991, midt i de intense intellektuelle diskussioner, der fandt sted på det 5. Alvar Aalto Symposium i Jyväskylä i Finland, lokkede jeg Steven til at tage med på en tur på 40 km for at besøge den enestående Petäjävesi Kirke, der blev bygget i 1764 af en lokal bygherre fra bondestanden. På vej til kirken fortalte jeg Steven, at den lokale menighed havde fremsendt en primitiv tegning af kirkens korsformede gulvplan til godkendelse hos det svenske hof (Finland var på den tid en del af Sverige), og at tegningen var blevet afvist og påført stemplet "uacceptabelt". Men på grund af de langsomme svartider på den tid havde landsbyboerne allerede færdiggjort kirken, da afslaget fra Stockholm nåede frem.

Nu er den ydmyge kirke et monument, der er beskyttet af UNESCO. Jeg tror, at de rørende dybfølte tømmerhvælvinger, der efterligner renæssancens stenstrukturer, beseglede vores venskab.

Holl havde bygget relativt små beboelsesejendomme og butiksinteriører indtil han i 1992 blev bedt om at skabe *Kiasma Museum of Contemporary Art* i Helsinki (1992–98) på grundlag af hans vindende bidrag til den internationale arkitektkonkurrence, der tiltrak sig et rekordhøjt antal på ikke mindre end 520 forslag. Men selv med den uigendrivelige autoritet, som konkurrencesejren bibragte, var designopgaven exceptionelt krævende såvel kontekstuelt som funktionelt, teknisk, og endog politisk. Ud over de sædvanlige arkitektoniske interesser skulle Holl også gøre sig fortrolig med kæmpefiguren af Marskal Mannerheim, hvis rytterstatue ved siden af museet førte til en ophidset offentlig debat om Holls museums egnethed på stedet; en debat, der næsten formåede at få projektet til at kuldsejle. Museumsprojektet føjede med sine komplekse problemstillinger og krav nye facetter til Holls arkitektoniske praksis.

Sideløbende med *Kiasma*-projektet arbejdede Holl og hans kontor også på to andre, lige så udfordrende projekter, nemlig *Cranbrook Institute of Science* i Bloomfield Hills, Michigan (1993–98), nærmere bestemt en udvidelse og renovering af det museum, som Eliel Saarinen tegnede i 1931 (som et kuriosum kan det nævnes, at *Kiasma* ligger blot en enkelt karré fra Eliel Saarinens storslåede *Helsinki Jernbanestation*); samt *Chapel of St. Ignatius* in Seattle (1994–97), den by, som han tilbragte sin barndom og ungdom i. Disse tre projekter fastslog Steven Holls position som en af vor tids mest innovative og flittige arkitekter. I disse sideløbende projekter udviklede han sin karakteristiske fornemmelse for integrerede rum, der rækker videre end tanken om blot at føje elementer sammen et efter et, og hans karakteristiske brug af reflekteret lys og farve, sanselig materialitet, og haptiske detaljer. Han finpudsede også sin personlige designmetodologi såvel som hans fremgangsmåde i samarbejdet med talrige assistenter og specialister. Hans praksis voksede sig hurtigt til et internationalt foretagende, der vandt talrige konkurrencer og opgaver i Europa, Nærøsten, Japan, Kina, Korea og Cambodja samt i mange byer i USA.

Holl har altid taget afstand fra tanken om en rationaliseret og instrumentaliseret praksis; forestillingen om en "corporate architecture" har stærkt negative overtoner i hans sprog. I stedet for at bruge rette linier, gentagne moduler og tilføjelse efter tilføjelse har han stræbt efter at skabe arkitektoniske helheder, og hans bygninger fremstår ofte som om de er udskåret eller støbt i ét stykke snarere end som sammenstykkede strukturer; egenskaber, der bibringer en fornemmelse af noget helstøbt, afsluttet og unikt, både når man ser på helheden og på enkeltelementerne. Hans flademønstre, for eksempel vinduer og væginddelinger – eller blot sammensætningen af skabsdøre og skuffer – danner ofte sammenhængende figurer, der fremmaner en visuel kohærens ikke ulig den visuelle helhed, der kendetegner Eduardo Chillidas

skulpturer. Holls brug af det gyldne snit som styrende princip i proportionerne underbygger denne fornemmelse af sammenhæng. "Proportioner føles snarere end de opfattes direkte. De er, ligesom kakofoni og harmoni i musik, ganske subjektive og ganske virkningsfulde," påpeger han.[3]

Holls insisterende og forsatte eksperimenteren, samt hans bevidste indsats for at undgå at låse sig fast i en bestemt karakteristisk stil, er gjort mulig af hans arbejdsmetode. Han kombinerer en subtil, kunstnerisk, intim og personlig søgen, foretaget ved hjælp af akvarelskitser, og brugen af poetiske verbale metaforer og stærke konceptuelle diagrammer (ofte udledt af videnskabelige begreber) med forlæg udført som fysiske modeller og, til sidst, computerskabte udviklings- og produktionstegninger. Computeren anvendes til at videreudvikle konceptet og skabe nøjagtige dokumenter, der understøtter dets udførelse; ikke til at skabe et formsprog eller formmæssigt udtryk. "Vi bruger computerstøttede teknikker i så godt som ethvert stadie af designprocessen, undtagen den indledende konceptfase. For mig må den første konceptskitse nødvendigvis begynde med en analog proces, der skaber en tæt sammenknytning af tanke, hånd og øje. Jeg føler, at man kun på denne måde kan være fuldstændigt forbundet med den rolle, som intuitionen spiller i den skabende fase med alle dens små facetter og særlige natur. I den første tegnefase føler jeg en direkte forbindelse til en åndelig betydning og til sammenføjningen af ide & rumudvikling. Derefter kan arbejdet tage fart digitalt. Processen kan føres videre ved hjælp af alle de lynhurtige computerbaserede redskaber, der findes [...]. I positiv forstand har de nye muligheder, som computerne giver, frisat vores designproces, så den kan være endnu mere fantasifuld."[4]

De tidlige arbejdsfasers fysiske og mentale intimitet og taktilitet, sammenføjet med arkitektens fænomenologiske interesse i lys, materialitet og detaljer, sikrer at den menneskelige hånds aftryk er til stede i mødet med den færdige bygning. Holls bygninger fremstår ofte med et bevidst råt skær, der står i modsætning til den sædvanlige glatte perfektion, der kendetegner nutidens avantgarde og minimalistiske arkitektur. Denne undgåelse af det fremstræbt perfekte i flader og finish skaber en fornemmelse af åbenhed; her føler man sig inviteret ind, hvorimod bygninger, der er besat af tanken om det perfekte, ofte udsender signaler om eksklusion og afvisning.

Steven Holl har formået at udvikle et exceptionelt overbevisende samspil af tanke og form, ide og skabelse, ord og materialer, teknologi og kunstnerisk udtryk. Arkitekters verbale filosofiske formuleringer står ofte i modsætning til deres egentlig designarbejde, men Holls fysiske former og skrevne ord er skabt ud fra de samme følelser, den samme materie; begge bygger på samspillet mellem perception, tanke og følelse. De opstår ikke ud af teoretiske overvejelser og logik, men ud af fantasi og en levet erfaring. I sin første bog, *Anchoring* (1989), anerkender Holl allerede denne grundlæggende dialektik inden for design, om end med en vis tøven: "Det skrevne sprogs relation til arkitektur frembyder kun et usikkert spejl, der kan holdes op som bevisførelse; det er snarere i en ordløs stilhed, at vi har de bedste chancer for at snuble vores vej ind i den zone af rum, lys og materie, som arkitekturen er. Selvom de ikke kan tjene som arkitektonisk bevis, frembyder ord et løfte. Værket er tvunget til at bære, hvad ordene ikke kan. Ord er pile, der peger i den rigtige retning; når de tages sammen, danner de et kort over arkitektoniske intentioner."[5]

Omkring et årti senere ser han den filosofiske afsøgnings rolle i et ganske klart lys: "En arkitektonisk filosofi, hvor afslappet eller tilfældig den end måtte være, driver værket hos enhver tænkende arkitekt. Det har været et løbende, livslangt projekt for mig at udvikle – sideløbende med mine opførte værker – et skriftligt vidnesbyrd om arkitekturens stræben som en form for tanke. Fra mit første lille manifest Anchoring, til vores fælles værk Questions of Perception (1993), har en arkitekturfilosofi været et det flygtige, aldrig helt opnåede mål. Glæden ved at bygge strukturer, der er drevet af større ideer, er et vidunderligt mysterium."[6]

Holl begyndte på et tidligt stadie at bruge sproglige og litterære koncepter til at styre og tilføje energi til sin designproces. Hans Berkovitz House i Martha's Vineyard i Massachusetts (1984) var inspireret af Herman Melvilles Moby Dick, eller, for at være helt præcis, af det afsnit i romanen, der berettede om hvordan den stamme af indianere, der oprindeligt beboede området, skabte en enestående form for bolig ved at udspænde huder eller bark over et hvalskelet, som de havde fundet på stranden. Holls hus på stranden er et metaforisk skelet, hvor den tætte træramme fungerer som hvalens ribben.

Holl navngav de forskellige husenheder i projektet Bridge of Houses for at skabe fornemmelsen af individuelle beboere og arkitektoniske fortællinger, alle særligt tilpassede de enkelte beboere: House of the Decider, House of the Doubter, House for a Man Without Opinions, The Riddle, Dream House, Four Tower House, Matter and Memory (Den Beslutsommes Hus, Tvivlerens Hus, Manden uden Meningers Hus, Gåden, Drømmehuset, Huset med de Fire Tårne, Materie og Hukommelse). De fiktive klienter, som han forestillede sig i forbindelse med sit projekt for Autonomous Artisans' Housing var: en papirhåndværker, træskærer/snedker, bådebygger, murermester, glasgravør, stukkatør og metalhåndværker. På tilsvarende vis var de imaginære klienter – "de fremmedes forbund" – i forbindelse med hans Hybrid Building i Florida som følger: tragiker, musiker og matematiker. Personificeringen af beboerne i et boligprojekt hjælper tilsyneladende til at bygge bro over anonymitetens fremmedgørende tomrum; en dybtfølende arkitekt forestiller sig det liv, der udspiller sig i de rum, han tegner; ikke blot deres geometriske og visuelle egenskaber. "Lad os forestille os en væg; hvad finder sted bag den?", er det råd, som digteren Jean Tardieu giver os arkiteter.[7] Alligevel har vi som oftest ikke tilstrækkelig interesse i at forestille os de liv, der udspiller sig i de huse, vi tegner.

Holls projekt for Knut Hamsun Centeret (1994-2009), der netop nu er i sin afsluttende fase i Hamarøy, Norge, bygger på et koncept, der er opstået ud fra litterære begreber i Hamsuns litteraturmesterværk Sult (1890). Det grundlæggende begreb om "usynlige kræfter" trækker på forfatterens halvt deliriske indrømmelser: "(Jeg var) saa fuldstændig et Bytte for sære, usynlige Indflydelser."[8] Arkitekten har medtaget andre scener fra romanen, f.eks. hvor "en Pige lagde sig ud af (vinduet) med opbrættede Ærmer og gav sig til at pudse Ruderne paa Ydersidena."[9]

Holl har også anvendt metaforer eller analogier fra musikken i sit arkitektoniske arbejde. Hans Stretto House i Dallas, Texas (1989–91) er baseret på musikkens begreb om 'stretto' (tæt føring eller øget tempo, bruges i fugaen for at akkompagnere sig selv og derved danne et kontrapunkt) og Béla Bartóks Musik for strengeinstrumenter, slagtøj og celeste. Musikkens fire satser, samt dens inddeling i slagtøj (det tunge) og strygere (det lette) afspejles i husets rumlige, formmæssige og materialemæssige strukturer. Et andet eksempel på inspiration fra musikken i Holls arbejde angår hans projekt for Sarphatistraat Kontorbygningerne i Amsterdam (1996–2000); lys og farver spejler sig, fanget bag perforerede metalfacader, og giver dermed mindelser om et koncept, der stammer fra Morton Feldmans komposition Patterns in a Chromatic Field.

Steven Holls fremmeste kreative redskab er hans koncepter, der er en kraftfuld sammenføjning af en metafor og en arkitektonisk idé i et enkelt styrende billede. Hans metaforiske designkoncepter som f.eks. Seven Bottles of Light in a Stone Box (Syv Flasker Med Lys i en Stenkasse) (Chapel of St. Ignatius); Strange Attractors, House of Vapor, Story of Water, Garden of Science, and House of Ice (Fraktal attraktor, Disens Hus, Vandets Historie, Videnskabens Have, og Isens Hus) (Addition to the Cranbrook Institute of Science); Tripleness and Right Hand Rule (Treenighed og Højrehåndet Overmagt) (Bellevue Art Museum (1997–2001), Menger Sponge (Mengers Svamp) (Sarphatistraat Offices), Porosity (Porøsitet) (Simmons Hall, 1999–2002), Stone and Feather (Sten og Fjer) (Nelson Atkins Museum, 1999–2007), og Writing with Light (Lysskrift) (Long Island, 2001–04) fremmaner alle poetiske eller videnskabelige billeder. Merleau-Pontys tanke om "kiasmen" (Helsinki Museum of Contemporary Art), som arkitekten anvendte som pejlemærke såvel som kodenavn for sit bidrag til konkurrencen, blev senere brugt som selve navnet på museet, Kiasma.[10]

Siden de tidligste trin af sin karriere har Holl arbejdet med en strategi, der angår et "begrænset koncept" ('limited concept'), der, som han skriver, "omformuleres til hvert enkelt sted og hver enkelt unikke program. […] Sproget bliver til et redskab, der muliggør 'genkendelsen af konceptet', således som de argumenteres for af Ernst Cassirer i dennes Philosophie der symbolishen Formen".[11] Han forklarer den afgørende rolle, som konceptuelle diagrammer spiller i hans arbejdsproces, således: "Jeg er aldeles afhængig af konceptdiagrammer. Jeg betragter dem som mit hemmelige våben. De gør det muligt for mig at bevæge sig friskt og uhæmmet fra et projekt til det næste, fra et sted til et andet. Hvis jeg gik til mine projekter med et fastfrosset vokabularium ville jeg have mistet min interesse i arkitektur for længe siden. Det at finde et udgangspunkt i et indledende koncept for hvert projekt; et koncept, der indfanger essensen af de arkitektoniske muligheder, der er unikke for netop det projekt, er for mig den dør, gennem hvilken nye ideer træder ind i arkitekturen. Selv om mange, om ikke det fleste, af de mennesker, der sætter pris på mit arbejde, synes at fokusere på dets eksperimenterende eller fænomenologiske egenskaber, på lyset, brugen af materialer, og så videre – så er ideen det vigtigste for mig."[12]

Holl udbygger sin arbejdsmetode yderligere i den samtale, vi havde i det spanske magasin *El Croquis* i 2002: "Et koncept er den 'motor', der giver designprocessen fremdrift. På et tidligt tidspunkt af hvert projekt, efter at vi har analyseret stedet og programmet, og undertiden efter adskillige mislykkedes startforsøg, beslutter vi os for et centralt koncept (eller koncepter) samt nogle vage rumlige skitser. Eftersom hvert eneste sted er unikt og har unikke forhold, sigter vi efter at skabe tilsvarende afbalancerede og stedsbestemte løsninger. Konceptet, der udtrykkes i et diagram og i ord, hjælper med til at skabe fokus i en række forskellige aspekter. Det er en hjælp i forbindelse med udviklingen af et projekt og kommunikationen med klienten [...] På sin vis er de individuelle 'poetiske noter' ikke blot motorer, der giver designet fremdrift – de er frisættende elementer, der knytter an til bredere tankegange inden for andre discipliner."[13]

Holls enestående åbenhed og modtagelighed i designprocessen kan eksemplificeres ved de runder af kritiske samtaler, han har om de igangværende projekter på sin tegnestue; her inviterer han ofte kritikere udefra i tilgift til sine ansatte. I løbet af design- og udviklingsfasen af *Kiasma*-projektet i Helsinki blev jeg ofte overrasket over hans åbenhed og evne til at acceptere klientens forslag eller krav, også selv om de nogen gange kunne forekomme urimelige og i modstrid med arkitektens oprindelige hensigter. Han var i stand til at omsætte sådanne hændelser til positive impulser i udviklingsprocessen i stedet for at betragte dem som uønskede forstyrrende elementer eller kompromiser.

Selv om Steven Holl er dybt engageret i en konceptuelt drevet designproces er han blandt de fremmeste repræsentanter for den fænomenologiske indgangsvinkel til arkitekturen i dag. Siden sine tidligste skrifter og tegninger har han fokuseret på de eksperimenterende og fænomeniske aspekter af arkitekturen, der opstår i det konkrete møde med værket. I stedet for de formmæssige spørgsmål, der primært behandles i nutidens arkitektoniske tankeverden, udforsker han de perceptuelle fænomener, der ligger implicit i forskellige aspekter af projektet, og han sigter efter ægte sansemæssige og mentale oplevelser, i særdeleshed efter bestemte taktile egenskaber, efter "den haptiske verden". Hans indledende, afsøgende fase med akvarellerne, såvel som den efterfølgende udvikling med de fysiske modeller, styrker materialets og den oplevede virkeligheds tilstedeværelse. Holl forklarer det

fænomenologiske grundlag for sit arbejde således: "Arkitekturen sammenfletter oplevelsen af tid, rum, lys og materialer, og eksisterer på et 'før-teoretisk grundlag'. Fænomenerne, der finder sted inden for et givent rum, såsom sollyset, der trænger ind gennem et vindue, eller en flades farver og genskin, står alle i et integreret forhold til hinanden inden for perceptionens verden. Membranens gennemskinnelighed, gipsens kalkagtige mathed, det blanke genskin af ugennemskinneligt glas og solstrålens lys flettes sammen i gensidigt givende forhold, der skaber den unikke oplevelse af et givent sted."[14]

I betragtning af Steven Holls engagement i malerkunsten siden sin tidlige ungdom, hans samarbejde med kunstnere, og hans lidenskabelige interesse i kunst er det ikke overraskende, at han er blevet en af de arkitekter, der nyder størst tillid, når det handler om at tegne nutidens museer.[15] Hans liste over projekter omfatter netop nu over et dusin konkurrencebidrag og opførte bygninger for kunstmuseer og andre udstillingssteder. Herudover har han arbejdet på næsten ti andre museumsprojekter, heriblandt museer for filmkunst og legetøj, naturhistorie, menneskets udvikling samt middelhavsområdets civilisationer.

Det seneste museum tegnet af Holl, *HEART Herning Museum of Contemporary Art,* er et frisat og selvsikkert projekt, der er udført af en erfaren skaber af rum for kunst. Idet bygningen ligger overfor en tidligere skjortefabrik (som museet midlertidig har haft ophold i), der er udformet som en skjortekrave, har Holl videreført det legende, Oldenburgske pop-art billede ved at tænke det nye museum som skjorteærmer, der krydser hinanden. De to egentlige udstillingsrum, "skattekisterne", er rationelt rektangulære rum, hvorimod stedets øvrige funktioner og faciliteter er arrangeret omkring denne rektangulære og funktionelt selvstændige kerne, hvor de følger frit formede konturer. Arkitekten understreger selv, at hans hensigt har været at tænke museet som en række rumlige oplevelser, der udmøntes ved samspillet mellem museets *parti pris* (overordnede idé) og de omkringliggende jordvolde snarere end ved at præsentere museet som et objekt i sig selv. Den sektionsvise strategi skaber en livlig rytme af udspændte sejlformer eller diagonale bølgeformer på tværs af og uafhængigt af plantegningen og skaber derved et skiftende dagslys i udstillingsrummene.

Da jeg ikke selv har besøgt *HEART,* må jeg afholde mig fra en yderligere beskrivelse af rummene og deres kendetegn; ethvert dybfølt arkitektonisk værk, der bevidst sigter efter et egentligt fysisk møde, kan kun opleves og bedømmes i selve "verdens kød", for nu at bruge et af de afgørende begreber hos en af Holls yndlingsfilosoffer, Maurice Merleau-Ponty.[16]

Mens konstruktionen af HEART har fundet sted er et andet af Steven Holls projekter i det nordiske, nemlig *Knut Hamsun Centeret* i Hamaroy tæt på forfatterens fødested, langt over polarcirklen i Norge, netop ved at gå ind i sin sidste byggefase efter femten års tøven. Dette projekt, der som omdrejningspunkt har Hamsun, en politisk kontroversiel litterær skikkelse, der vandt nobelprisen i 1920, viser tydeligt Holls fantasi og empati. Projektet sammenføjer en fornemmelse for det særligt norske formsprog med et surrealistisk og uheldssvangert billedsprog, der er aldeles egnet til formålet, men den drømmeagtige stemning synes også at forny arkitektens forbindelse med den noget surrealistiske stemning, der kendetegnede hans tidligste projekter. Gennem små forskydninger og forvrængninger (et umærkeligt hældende, tilsyneladende ustabilt tårn med "hår" på taget) fremmaner Holl en følelse af noget mystisk og ekstraordinært, der opstår ud af billeder, der på samme tid fremstår velkendte. Det sorte tårn hæver sig, både trygt og urovækkende, blandt de nordnorske traditionelle rødmalede huse med deres karakteristiske tage af tørv; samtidig indgår tårnet også i en dialog med de omkringliggende bjerge. Bygningen forholder sig til sin nordlige placering med vinduerne øverst, der tillader sollyset at trænge hele vejen ned til stueplanet, når det står i sin højeste vinkel på 47°. Holls projekt bærer vidnesbyrd om, at arkitekturen kan fortælle historier, og om at den kan gøre livets vilkår poetiske, give det tilsyneladende meningsløse mening, og afsløre de mysterier, der ligger bag vores hverdag.

"Vi [...] beskæftiger os med at udforske de grundlæggende oplevelser i dagligdagens fænomener. Ordinære og ekstraordinære fakta, omstændigheder og oplevelser kan, når de betragtes som vigtige, skabe en betydningsfuld arkitektur."[17]

Noter/ Kilder:

1 Projektet blev udført i samarbejde med Richard Meier and Partners, Eisenman Architects, samt Gwathmey Siegel & Associates Architects.
2 Udstillingen *Steven Holl/Emilio Ambasz,* Museum of Modern Art, New York, februar–april, 1989.
3 "A conversation with Steven Holl: Thought, Matter and Experience" (med Juhani Pallasmaa). *El Croquis* N. 108, 2002, s. 24.
4 "A conversation with Steven Holl", ibid., s. 25.
5 *Anchoring*, ibid., s. 9.
6 "A conversation with Steven Holl", ibid., s. 12.
   Holl henviser her til "Questions of Perception: Phenomenology of Architecture; *A + U Special Issue* (juli 1994), forfattet sammen med Alberto Pérez Gómez and Juhani Pallasmaa.
7 Citeret i Georges Perec, *Tiloja avaruuksia* [Espéces d'espaces]. Loki-kirjat, Helsinki, 1992, p. 72.
8 Knut Hamsun, *Sult*, Gerald Duckworth & Company, London, 1974, s. 15. (Da. P. G. Philipsens Forlag, København, 1890)
9 Op. cit..
10 Merleau-Ponty beskriver begreberne om sammenfletningen og kiasmen i sit essay "The Intertwining – The Chiasm" i *The Visible and the Invisible*, red. Claude Lefort, Northwestern University Press, Evanston, Illinois, fjerde oplag, 1992. (Da. "Synligt-Usynligt, i *Om sprogets fænomenologi – udvalgte tekster*, Samlerens bogklub 1999)
11 "A conversation with Steven Holl", ibid., s. 12.
12 Steven Holl, *Idea and Phenomena.* Lars Müller Publisher, Baden, 2002, s. 73. Citeret i Yehudi E. Safran, "Steven Holl: Idea and Method", *El Croquis* Nr 93, Madrid 1999.
13 "A conversation with Steven Holl", ibid., s. 16.
14 Steven Holl, *arc en rêve centre d'architecture.* Artemis Verlag, Zurich, 1994, s. 3.
15 Holls bror er maler, og Steven begyndte selv at male i 1959 inden han blev interesseret i arkitektur. Allerede som 12-årig udstillede han sine malerier på Kitsap Country Fair i staten Washington. Holl medgiver selv, at hans møder med Donald Judd, Dennis Oppenheim, Richard Nonas, Meg Webster, James Turrell og andre kunstnere i tiden i New York efter 1976 havde afgørende betydning for udviklingen af hans arkitektoniske tanker.
   "A conversation with Steven Holl", ibid., s 8.
   I sine mange projekter har Holl arbejdet sammen med førende kunstnere såsom Vito Acconci og Walter de Maria.
16 Merleau-Ponty beskriver tanken om "kødet" i sit essay "The Intertwining – the Chiasm" i Claude Lefort, red. *The Visible and the Invisible.* Northwestern University Press, Evanston, Illinois, 1969. (Da. "Sammenfletningen – Kiasmen" i "Synligt–Usynligt", i *Om sprogets fænomenologi – udvalgte tekster*, Samlerens bogklub 1999)
17 Steven Holl, "Foreword", *Intertwining,* Princeton Architectural Press, New York, 1996, s. 7.

heart

Holger Reenberg

Der Wettbewerb 1

Als ich im Frühjahr 2005 zum ersten Mal den Raum im Herning Kunstmuseum betrat, in dem die Tafeln mit den Wettbewerbsbeiträgen anonym ausgestellt waren, zog mich ein Entwurf ganz besonders in den Bann und ließ mich nicht mehr los. In den folgenden Monaten tagte in diesem Raum, der Stein-Raum genannt wird, die dreizehnköpfige Jury, die damit beauftragt war, den richtigen Entwurf für ein neues Gebäude für das Herning Kunstmuseum auszusuchen.

Der Entwurf, der mir besonders gut gefiel, war ganz in Schwarz-Weiß gestaltet und offensichtlich von Hand gemacht! Damit meine ich, dass die Bilder von dem Gebäude keine dreidimensionalen Visualisierungen waren, die mit dem Computer erstellt wurden, sondern körperlicher Natur waren, das heißt, sie zeigten ein tatsächliches Modell. Die Bilder auf den Tafeln waren abwechselnd Fotos eines Architekturmodells, Handzeichnungen und der Aquarelle. Mit ein klein wenig Ironie könnte man fast sagen, dass diese Präsentation ein Traum für einen Kunsthistoriker war, aber das war beileibe nicht alles, was für diesen Entwurf sprach: Die Tafeln riefen eine Reihe formaler und materieller Assoziationen hervor, die genau zur Lage, Geschichte und Kunst des Museums passten.

Damgaard, Gadegaard und Manzoni

Seit seiner Eröffnung im Jahr 1977 war das Herning Kunstmuseum im Angli-Gebäude, der Hemdenfabrik, die Aage Damgaard erbaut hat, untergebracht. Zu dieser Zeit hatte die Familie Damgaard mittels ihres Midtjysk Skole- og Kulturfond (Mitteljütländische Stiftung für Bildung und Kultur) bereits die Hauptwerke aus Aage Damgaards außergewöhnlichen Kunstsammlung dem dänischen Staat gestiftet, um ein staatlich anerkanntes Museum gründen zu können. Aage Damgaard stellte in den Räumlichkeiten, in denen später das Herning Kunstmuseum untergebracht werden sollte, zunächst Hemden her. Im Rahmen seiner Hemdenfabrik förderte er die Zusammenarbeit von Vertretern der Geschäftswelt und Künstlern, die zum damaligen Zeitpunkt in Dänemark recht einzigartig war und es bis heute noch ist.

Diese Kooperation bildet auch die historische und konzeptionelle Grundlage für die Biennale Socle du Monde, die erstmals 2002 stattfand und von HEART in Zusammenarbeit mit der ortsansässigen Vereinigung von Geschäftsleuten, Erhvervsrådet, veranstaltet wird.

In einem Brief, den er im Sommer 1960 auf dem Briefpapier des Herning Missionshotels an einen Freund verfasste, schrieb Piero Manzoni, dass er von der Angli-Fabrik angestellt wurde und einen Assistenten mit einem Auto zur Verfügung gestellt bekommen hatte. Aage Damgaard war von dem Maler Paul Gadegaard auf Manzoni aufmerksam gemacht worden. Damals arbeitete Gadegaard gerade an der Innenausstattung von Damgaards neuem Fabrikgebäude, bekannt als »die schwarze Fabrik«. Tatsächlich war die Fassade des Gebäudes tiefschwarz, aber im Innern waren alle Böden, Wände und Decken in hellen, leuchtenden Farben und mit abstrakten Formen bemalt. Paul Gadegaard hatte freie Hand, ein Gesamtinterieur zu schaffen, ein dekoratives Gestaltungskonzept von bisher unbekannten Ausmaßen. Man könnte sagen, dass der Traum, die Kunst solle die sozialen Räume erobern – ein Traum, den eine ganze Generation träumte –, seinen Höhepunkt in Gadegaards Arbeit in Herning in der Zeit von 1952 bis 1982 erreichte.

Im folgenden Sommer 1961 besuchte Manzoni Herning erneut, und wieder war es ihm ganz frei überlassen, welche eigenen künstlerischen Ziele er verfolgen wollte. Mit dem Resultat, dass das Herning Kunstmuseum nun sechsundvierzig Arbeiten von Manzoni, unter ihnen *La linea lunga* (1960) und *Socle du monde* (1961), besitzt.

Der Arbeit des Herning Kunstmuseums liegen zwei Schwerpunkte zugrunde. Einer ist die Sammlung von Werken Piero Manzonis. Es ist die größte öffentliche Sammlung ihrer Art weltweit, und jedes Jahr gibt es Leihanfragen von Museen aus aller Welt. Der zweite Schwerpunkt steht im Zusammenhang mit den Anfängen der ständigen Sammlung, also der Privatsammlung des Hemdenfabrikanten Aage Damgaard und der einzigartigen Weise, auf die diese Sammlung begründet wurde. Im Laufe der letzen sieben Jahre hat das Museum daran gearbeitet, diese beiden Schwerpunkte wirksam einzusetzen, indem es die Manzoni-Sammlung und Aage Damgaards einzigartige Form des Mäzenatentums Teil des Konzepts werden ließ, in Verbindung mit allen Veranstaltungen und Ausstellungen.

Zwar konnte das Museum Werke von Manzoni an andere Institutionen ausleihen, es konnte aber nie Ausstellungen mit Gegenleihgaben zeigen. Hauptsächlich, weil das Gebäude, eine alte Fabrikhalle, im Hinblick auf die äußeren Bedingungen als Ausstellungsort untauglich war. So konnte das Museum nie Ausstellungen organisieren, die der Qualität der eigenen Sammlung entsprochen hätten. Wenn das Museum beispielsweise Arbeiten von Manzoni an das Guggenheim Museum in New York auslieh, konnte das Angebot einer entsprechenden Leihgabe von Wassily Kandinsky aus der Guggenheim-Sammlung nicht angenommen werden.

Der Wettbewerb 2
Diese Geschichte – und dieses Stück Kunstgeschichte – wurde auf direkte und doch schwer fassbare Weise von den schwarzen und weißen Tafeln im Stein-Raum hervorgerufen. Der Schwerpunkt des Entwurfs lag eindeutig auf dem, was der Gründer des Louisiana Museum of Modern Art in Dänemark, Knud W. Jensen, als »Genius Loci«, den Geist des Ortes, bezeichnet hat. Dieser wurde nicht durch eine kluge Architekturmetapher oder eine offenkundig symbolische Form erreicht, obwohl Symbolismus und Metaphern bedeutende Bestandteile des Ganzen waren. In gewisser Hinsicht schien

sich das Gebäude selbst als eine natürliche Fortsetzung seiner tatsächlichen Umgebung heraufzubeschwören. Gleichzeitig verband es eine klare Funktionalität, die den Ausstellungsanforderungen gerecht wurde, mit einem poetischen Gefühl für die Kunst, die in dem Gebäude untergebracht werden sollte. Was ich damals noch nicht wusste, aber was ich mir vielleicht hätte denken können, war, dass der Name des Architekten Steven Holl war.

Aus meiner Zeit am Arken Museum of Modern Art in Kopenhagen war ich zu einem gewissen Grad mit der Architektur von Steven Holl vertraut. Durch meine damalige Position an diesem Museum sprach ich häufig mit Tuula Arkio und Maretta Jaukuuri, die damals Direktorin beziehungsweise leitende Kuratorin am Kiasma Museum of Contemporary Art in Helsinki waren, einem Gebäude, das Holl entworfen hat. Ich hörte von ihrer Zusammenarbeit und besuchte die Baustelle, um das Fortschreiten des Projektes zu beobachten, ein Projekt, das große Funktionalität und Respekt vor der Kunst mit einer ausdrucksstarken Architektursprache verband. Nach meiner Ankunft in Herning tauchte Holls Name immer wieder in Gesprächen zwischen Lars Damgaard, dem Sohn von Aage Damgaard, und mir auf.

Der Wettbewerb wurde am 16. Februar 2005 ausgelobt. Es wurde beschlossen, dass sechs Architekten daran teilnehmen durften, von denen vier durch Vorqualifizierungsrunden ermittelt und die anderen beiden eingeladen werden sollten, ihre Entwürfe einzureichen. Das Feld der endgültigen Teilnehmer umfasste die Architekturbüros CUBO und 3XNielsen – beide aus Århus, Dänemark – sowie Snøhetta aus Oslo und Keith Williams Architects aus London. Steven Holl Architects aus New York und Caruso St John aus London wurden ausdrücklich zur Teilnahme eingeladen. Es war ein wunderbares Gefühl, endlich das Stadium zu erreichen, in dem der tatsächliche Wettbewerb (30. Mai bis 9. September 2005) beginnen konnte und man auf Beiträge von derart guten Architekten wartete. Vor allem aber war es sehr befriedigend, dass wir die Stiftung Realdania gefunden hatten, die an unser Projekt glaubte und es finanziell unterstützen würde. Zum damaligen Zeitpunkt war ich bereits seit vier Jahren Direktor des Herning Kunstmuseums, und meine Hauptaufgabe war es, ein neues Museumsgebäude entstehen zu lassen.

2001–2005
Im Jahr 2000 bat mich der neue Aufsichtsratsvorsitzende des Herning Kunstmuseums, Lars Damgaard, um ein Gespräch. Lars Damgaard war gleichzeitig Chef der Restaurantkette A Hereford Beefstouw, die sein Vater gegründet hatte. Der Termin dauerte nicht lange, und Lars Damgaards Wunsch war eindeutig: Das Herning Kunstmuseum sollte einen Neubeginn wagen, und dieser sollte mit einem neuen Gebäude einhergehen! Zahlreiche Vorstellungsgespräche mit dem Aufsichtsrat fanden in dichter Folge statt, und im März 2001 trat ich meine neue Stelle als Museumsdirektor in Herning an. Wenn ein Bauprojekt wie Steven Holls Entwurf jemals in einer kleinen Stadt realisiert werden soll, muss der Zeitpunkt

genau richtig gewählt sein. Es wäre allerdings verzeihlich, ein bisschen Lokalpatriotismus an den Tag zu legen und zu fragen, welcher Moment in Herning nicht genau richtig wäre? Denn Herning ist für seinen Unternehmungsgeist, seine Initiative und vor allem für seine Fähigkeit zur Kooperation über politische und berufliche Grenzen hinweg, um großartige Resultate zu erzielen, gut bekannt: Resultate, die sonst für eine kleine dänische Stadt außer Reichweite wären. Und trotzdem verlangte diese Herausforderung nach etwas Besonderem. Das Museum hatte sich bereits zweimal erfolglos bemüht, ein neues Bauprojekt zu realisieren.

Das Projekt war bereits vor meiner Ankunft auf einem guten Weg zur Realisierung. Johannes Jensen, der Gründer und Leiter der örtlichen Teppichfirma Wilton Tæpper und mittlerweile leider verstorben, hatte der Gemeinde Herning mit der strengen Auflage, dass es für ein neues Kunstmuseum verwendet werden musste, ein Stück Land geschenkt. Darüber hinaus war dem Aufsichtsrat des Museums durch den Beitritt neuer Mitglieder frischer Lebensgeist eingehaucht worden.

Lars Damgaard, Johannes Poulsen, Mitglied des dänischen Parlaments und des örtlichen Gemeinderats, und ich selbst arbeiteten von Anfang an eng und erfolgreich zusammen. Im Jahr 2002 wurde Lars Krarup neuer Bürgermeister von Herning, und sein großes Engagement für unser Projekt hatte einen entscheidenden Einfluss auf die Fertigstellung.

Im Jahr 2002 gab es eine Reihe erster Kontakte und Entscheidungen wurden getroffen. In diesem Jahr legten wir einen Kurs fest, der sich als richtig herausstellen sollte. Gemeinsam mit dem Erhvervsrådet rief das Herning Kunstmuseum die alle zwei Jahre stattfindende Socle du Monde ins Leben. Der Biennale liegt die Idee der Zusammenarbeit von Künstlern und Vertretern der Geschäftswelt zugrunde, und sie ist somit ganz im Geiste von Aage Damgaard angelegt, gekennzeichnet durch vollständige künstlerische Freiheit. Etwa zur gleichen Zeit entschieden die Gemeinde von Herning und das Museum, dass das gerade gegründete lokale Orchester MidWest Ensemble ebenfalls im neuen Museum untergebracht werden sollte – falls es jemals realisiert werden würde.

Wir stellten außerdem den Kontakt zu Henning Kruse Petersen her, der damals Chef des Finanzinstituts Nykredit war. Kruse Petersen sollte später Mitglied des Aufsichtsrats und der Verantwortliche für das Fundraising des Bauprojektes werden. Er brachte sein weitreichendes Netzwerk und eine neue Dynamik, die sich auf den Prozess auswirkte, mit. Entscheidend war auch, dass wir unsere ersten Treffen mit der Realdania-Stiftung arrangierten und ihr Interesse soweit wecken konnten, dass sie beschloss, eine Machbarkeitsstudie zu finanzieren, die von PLS Rambøll ausgeführt wurde. Rambøll legte Anfang 2004 eine Studie vor, die das Vorhaben als positiv auswies. Unter anderem zeigte die Studie, dass die wichtigste Voraussetzung für den Erfolg des Projektes die Manzoni-Sammlung des Herning Kunstmuseums war. Auf Grundlage dieser Studie entschied sich Realdania, die Gelder für einen Architekturwettbewerb zur Verfügung zu stellen.

HEART

Es gibt eine Architektur, die auf dem Bildschirm oder der Leinwand gut aussieht, die aber nie ihren Weg auf ein richtiges Baugrundstück finden sollte; und dann gibt es eine Architektur, die von Menschen für Menschen und für die Welt entworfen wurde. Im Laufe der letzten beiden Jahrzehnte haben wir den Bau vieler neuer Kunstmuseen erlebt, deren Architektur für sich genommen interessant sein mag, die aber als Kunstmuseen oder sogar als Ausstellungsräume vollständig ungeeignet sind. Natürlich ist das zu einem gewissen Grad eine Frage des Geschmacks. Alles hängt davon ab, was für eine Art von Museum wir haben möchten, welche Rolle es übernehmen soll und wie man Kunst ausstellen möchte.

Wenn man Kuratoren und Museumsdirektoren vom »White Cube« sprechen hört, vom anonymen, flexiblen, rechteckigen Raum als der einzig wahren Lösung für Ausstellungsräume, scheint es, als würde man den zugrunde liegenden Wunsch heraushören, Museumsarchitektur möge sich nicht verändern oder weiterentwickeln. Die Forderung nach einem anonymen Ausstellungsraum steht mit der Vorstellung von Kunst als etwas Autonomem in Verbindung. Der Ausdruck »ein autonomes Kunstwerk« an sich verrät bereits eine Art der Betrachtung, dass Kunst eine einzigartige Qualität hat, etwas, das über allen Dingen und tatsächlich über allem anderen steht. In gewisser Hinsicht postuliert diese Auffassung auch, dass ein Meisterwerk in vollkommener Unabhängigkeit von allen äußeren Faktoren als solches geschätzt und erkannt werden kann. Das stimmt natürlich nicht – jedenfalls nicht ganz!

Nicht jedes beliebige Werk kann von allen als Kunst erkannt werden. Die Anerkennung dieser Tatsache ist ein wichtiger Faktor für die Bestimmung der Möglichkeiten der Kunstmuseen, in einen Dialog mit den Besuchern zu treten. Wenn das Kunstwerk während des Prozesses seiner Entstehung, seiner Wahrnehmung und seiner Erkennung von so vielen verschiedenen Faktoren abhängt, warum sollte es dann nicht auch vom Raum abhängig sein? Und, wenn das wahr ist, warum sollte es dann immer von einem weißen, anonymen Raum bestimmt werden, der, wenn man dies logisch zu Ende denkt, schließlich zu einer Art globaler Corporate Identity wird?

Meiner Meinung nach muss es bei der Diskussion um das autonome Kunstwerk und den Ausstellungsraum nicht um ein »Entweder-oder« gehen. Kunstmuseen können in Kirchen, Dörfern, auf einsamen Stränden, in Einkaufszentren oder auf Bergpässen gebaut werden, und man kann in ihnen alles ausstellen, was man möchte.

Einerseits müssen wir akzeptieren, dass heute sowohl das Innere als auch das Äußere des Museums an einem starken und widersprüchlichen Dialog mit der es umgebenden Gesellschaft teilnehmen. Mit dieser Herausforderung muss umgegangen werden, zusammen mit den vielen Sozialleistungen – und Risiken, den Kern des Museums zu verderben –, die damit einhergehen. Andererseits könnten wir behaupten, dass einige der Werke, die schließlich in ein Museum gelangen – das eine historische Institution ist und es auch bleiben sollte – zu einem gewissen Grad ein unabhängiges Leben erreicht haben, eine Art von unangreifbarem Status, zumindest eine Zeit lang. Innerhalb dieser Zeit und dieses Raums können wir gelegentlich damit experimentieren, sie von den gegenwärtigen Absichten der Verbrauchergesellschaft und der Politik zu lösen.

Im Ausschreibungstext für den Wettbewerb nannten wir es das »offene Schatzkästchen«. Ein Haus mit einer Umgebung, die offen und einladend ist, während seine inneren Kammern echte Schätze beherbergen und im Widerspruch zur äußeren Offenheit stehen. Den Gewinner zu finden, wurde eine langwierige und manchmal auch schwierige Aufgabe, aber am 14. Oktober 2005 konnten wir ihn schließlich verkünden: Es war das Projekt von Steven Holl. Der erste Spatenstich fand am 25. Juni 2007 statt.

Als der Gewinner bekannt gegeben wurde, kommentierte Steen Høyer, Professor und Landschaftsarchitekt, dies in der dänischen Architekturzeitschrift *Arkitekten* wie folgt: »Man sieht heutzutage nur noch selten, dass begabte Architekten sich selbst und ihre Aufgabe ernst nehmen, ohne dass das Projekt angeberisch wirkt oder einen kommerziellen Charakter hat [...]. Der Eigentümer des Gebäudes wünscht sich, eine gewisse Ernsthaftigkeit in Bezug auf die Kunst zu bewahren. Ein fester, ausdrucksstarker Rahmen, der für sich selbst steht, ohne ein aggressiver oder neunmalkluger Gegner zu sein [...]. Die meisten Architekten betrachten Kunst als eine Ware, die einen Teil der demokratischen Landschaft bildet und auf der üblichen Marktlage beruht. Im Gegensatz dazu wünscht sich dieser Gebäudeeigentümer, dass die Einzigartigkeit der Kunstwerke durch ein würdevolles Gebäude in Birk erhalten wird.«

Jetzt stehen an beiden Enden des Birk Centerparks Strukturen mit auffällig skulpturalen Qualitäten, die jedoch grundsätzlich sehr verschieden sind. Das eine ist Ingvar Crohammars *Elia,* eingeweiht im Jahr 2001: das Werk eines Mystikers ohne Sinn oder Zweck, das die nützlichen Anstrengungen des weißen Geschäftsparks leugnet und auslöscht. Die andere Struktur ist Steven Holls neues – und ja, weißes – Museumsgebäude, das HEART heißt.

Der Name und die visuelle Identität mit der ausdrucksstarken Schrift entstanden 2007 durch die Type »Kontrapunkt«.

Wie alle Gebäude von Steven Holl ist auch HEART genau für diesen bestimmten Ort entworfen worden, in diesem Fall, um als Museum zu dienen. Die Assoziationen und Verweise, die ich instinktiv bei meinem ersten Betrachten der Wettbewerbstafeln wahrnahm, entstanden zunächst durch die Fassaden mit ihrer funktionalen Geometrie, die sie sich zu eigen gemacht hatten, und durch die anthropomorphe Ausdruckskraft der Dachstruktur. Das Verhältnis zwischen dem Organischen und dem Geometrischen fungiert als eine Paraphrase der konkreten Kunst von Paul Gadegaard, der in den Stoffresten der Hemdenfabrikation in Angli seinen Ausgangspunkt gesehen zu haben scheint.

Die Thematik von HEART betrifft die Haptik und die Materialität. Die äußeren Wände sind auf der Baustelle geformt worden, sie bestehen aus weißem Beton und begrüßen uns mit einer zerknitterten, textilartigen Oberfläche. Diese Verweise auf den Tastsinn (und Textiles) werden beim Dach, das den Grundriss bestimmt, weitergeführt. Das Dach besteht aus fünf Planen, die an die Ärmel von Hemden erinnern, die längs geschnitten sind. Die Ärmel rufen starke Assoziationen zu den aufsteigenden Planen des Utzon-Hauses hervor. Mit seinen leichten, zerknitterten Wänden und hängenden Ärmeln sieht HEART wie ein Zelt aus Beton aus.

Die ärmelartige Dachstruktur umfasst auch zwei zurückspringende Flachdächer. Die Ärmel und die Oberflächen werden von einem vertikalen Band aus sandgestrahlten Glasfenstern verbunden, das die Ausstellungsräume mit Licht versorgt.

Das eigentliche Zentrum des Grundrisses sind zwei Ausstellungsräume; ihre rechtwinklige Gradlinigkeit wehrt sich gegen den organischen Charakter der Decken. Das übergeordnete Konzept des Grundrisses – dass die Ausstellungsräume rechteckige und quadratische Räume innerhalb eines »überdachten Rechtecks« bilden, die von den anderen Funktionen innerhalb der äußeren Hülle des Gebäudes umgeben sind – steht im Einklang mit den Ausschreibungsanforderungen in Bezug auf eine grundsätzliche Offenheit in Verbindung mit dem Konzept der »Schatzkästchen«.

Die Sprache von HEART ist kein autoritäres Architekturidiom, das beliebig eingesetzt wurde, um einen Ort zu erschaffen, der sich von anderen unterscheiden sollte, einen Ort, an dem Wirtschaft, Politik und Lifestyle die wichtigsten Parameter sind oder sein werden. Im Gegenteil: Das Gebäude ist zum einen so geformt, dass es in eine Verbindung zu seinen Nachbarn tritt – Jørn Utzons prototypischem Haus und der Angli-Fabrik –, und zum anderen so, dass es sich auf die Geschichte bezieht, die diesen Ort und diese einzigartige Kunstsammlung, die HEART beherbergt, geprägt hat.

monochrom

Steven Holl

Nemtschinowka

Da es unsere erste Moskaureise war, wollten wir gerne den Grabstein von Kasimir Malewitsch in Nemtschinowka sehen, den wir von Fotografien kannten: ein weißer Kubus mit einem schwarzen Quadrat. Wir korrespondierten per E-Mail mit unseren Architektenfreunden Prof. Vladimir und Ludmilla Kirpichev und baten sie, diesen Besuch in unsere Reiseplanung einzubeziehen. Ludmilla erklärte uns, dass der Grabstein und auch die große Eiche, unter der er gestanden hatte, im Zweiten Weltkrieg zerstört worden waren. Sie schrieb: »Nach Nemtschinowka zu gehen bedeutet, nirgendwo hin zu gehen.« Meine Frau, die Künstlerin Solange Fabião, erwiderte sofort: »Dann müssen wir unbedingt dorthin!«

Seit Mitte der 1970er-Jahre, als ich seine Gemälde *Weißes Quadrat auf weißem Grund* von 1918 und *Schwarzes Quadrat* von 1915 und seine Schriften zum Suprematistischen Manifest entdeckt habe, war ich von Malewitschs Werk besessen. Nach meiner Ankunft in New York im Jahr 1977 waren vier Jahre lang alle Zeichnungen, die ich machte, schwarz-weiß. Solange war seit ihrer Zeit an der Berliner Akademie der Künste und der Freien Universität von 1986 bis 1988 von Malewitsch fasziniert.

An einem sonnigen Morgen im März brachen wir gemeinsam in einem Mietwagen auf und fuhren von Moskau in Richtung Nemtschinowka. Unter einem klaren blauen Himmel sah man noch einzelne Schneeflecken. Nachdem wir ein paar Stunden gefahren waren, erreichten wir eine Ansammlung relativ neuer Datschen und entdeckten dort eine Straße, die »Malewitsch« hieß. Wir bogen in eine Straße ein, auf der rechts und links noch der Schnee schmolz, und kamen bald

darauf bei einer Lichtung an. Dort stand ein großer weißer Kubus mit einem roten Quadrat. Darauf stand geschrieben: »Hier ist der Ort, an dem mein Vater begraben ist, wie ich in ihn Erinnerung habe.« Der rekonstruierte Kubus war von Malewitschs Tochter 1989, ein Jahr bevor sie selbst starb, errichtet worden. Vladimir und Ludmilla standen ungläubig da, während Solange und ich begeistert waren, diese Stelle in Nemtschinowka entdeckt zu haben. Später fanden wir die grüne, mit einer Bronzeplakette gekennzeichnete Holzdatsche, in der Malewitsch immer die Sommer verbracht hatte.

Monochrom, achrom, Malewitsch & Manzoni

Wenn wir an die sechsundvierzig Originale von Piero Manzoni im HEART Herning Museum of Contemporary Art denken, könnten wir zurückschauen: Von den monochromen Obsessionen und Schriften von Kasimir Malewitsch gibt es eine geistige Verbindung zu den achromen Werken von Piero Manzoni.

Holger Reenberg hat über die Verbindungen zwischen Malewitsch und Manzoni, der »den Nullpunkt erreichen wollte, von dem aus alles möglich ist«, geschrieben. Obwohl ich Piero Manzoni gekannt hatte, erfuhr ich erst durch die ausführliche Broschüre, die im Zusammenhang mit dem Wettbewerb für das Herning Center of the Arts entstanden war, dass viele seiner wichtigsten Arbeiten in Herning, Dänemark, entstanden waren. Dieser Ort in Mitteljütland schien mit der geheimnisvollen Energie der Arte Povera, der Künstlergruppe Zero und dem monochromen Wüstengrund von Malewitsch aufgeladen zu sein.

Wir gehörten zu den sechs Architekten, die eingeladen worden waren, an dem Wettbewerb für das neue Herning Center of the Arts, das neben der ursprünglichen Hemdenfabrik lag, in der nun das Museum untergebracht war, teilzunehmen. Der Grundriss des Gebäudes aus den

1960er-Jahren hatte die Form eines Hemdkragens. Herning war ein interessanter, ganz besonderer Ort. Obwohl wir die Ausschreibungsunterlagen bereits im April oder Mai bekommen hatten, begannen wir erst später mit der Arbeit an dem Wettbewerb, weil wir im Büro mit so vielen anderen Aufgaben und Wettbewerben beschäftigt waren. (In diesem Sommer des Jahres 2005 haben wir drei Wettbewerbe in Folge, unter anderem das Knokke-Heist-Hotel in Belgien und die Cité du surf et de l'océan in Biarritz, mit Solange Fabião, gewonnen.) Ende August las ich dann die Ausschreibungsunterlagen erneut und akzeptierte begeistert die vorgeschlagenen Baubeschränkungen von einer Höhenbegrenzung auf acht Meter und der Festlegung auf die Farbe Weiß.

Ich beschäftigte mich lange mit Piero Manzonis Arbeiten, um mich in den Wettbewerb einzufühlen. Seine Arbeit *Socle du monde* hatte mich vor Jahren inspiriert, als ich mich mit den Arbeiten von Robert Smithson, Michael Heizer und anderen Konzeptkünstlern, die mit Land arbeiten, beschäftigte. Piero Manzoni war ihnen allen mit der Arbeit *Socle du monde*, die in Herning entstanden ist, vorausgegangen. Verschiedene Experimente mit Textilien aus der *Achrome*-Reihe waren auch in der Fabrik in Herning entstanden. Als eine Verbindung zu diesen Werken entwarfen wir das Gebäude in weißen Betonplatten, deren Formen angelegt waren, um wie Falten von Textilien auszusehen.

Es war ein Zufall, dass ausgerechnet mein dänischer Lieblingsarchitekt Jørn Utzon eines seiner prototypischen Gebäude von 1972 neben dem Gelände des Museum erbaut hatte. Es diente nun als Wohnhaus und war in hervorragend gepflegtem Zustand, und seine Beziehung zu dem Neubau war für unsere anfänglichen Überlegungen sehr wichtig.

Schatzkästchen / Hemdsärmel
Als nur noch etwas über eine Woche Zeit war, verbrachte ich das Wochenende damit, Skizzen zu einem Konzept zu machen. Ich beschloss, die Galerien als zwei »Schatzkästchen« zu verstehen – Rechtecke in der Mitte des Grundrisses, die dann locker verteilte, geschwungene Dachelemente haben würden, um das Licht zu sammeln. Die flache, ungestaltete Landschaft war teilweise in die Gegenrichtung der Geometrie des Daches geformt und verband so die Architektur mit der Landschaft. Von oben betrachtet sehen die Formen aus wie die Ärmel von Hemden, die auf Kisten geworfen wurden. An den freien Kanten des Grundrisses konnten ein Café, ein Hörsaal und eine Eingangshalle untergebracht werden, und die rechtwinkligen Ausstellungsräume konnten einzeln geschlossen werden, damit der Lehrkörper sie außerhalb der Öffnungszeiten benutzen konnte. Auf einem einzigen Geschoss würde das Gebäude eine hervorragende Luftzirkulation haben und geothermisch beheizt und gekühlt werden.

Dies erschien mir als interessantes Konzept, weil es direkten Bezug auf die Lage des Gebäudes nahm. Die Innenräume sollten durch ein graduiertes, geschwungenes Licht belebt werden. Als ich am Montagmorgen ins Büro kam, fragte ich

drei meiner Assistenten, ob sie in der verbleibenden Woche vor dem Abgabetermin eine Präsentation erarbeiten könnten. Nach einem begeisterten »Ja!« konnten wir den Abgabetermin einhalten, indem wir einige der Nächte durcharbeiteten. Die Präsentationstafeln mit den Schwarz-Weiß-Fotografien des kleinen Modells sahen fantastisch aus. Ich stellte mir vor, dass es in den rechtwinkligen Galerien ein Licht von unglaublicher Qualität gibt. In plakativen Diskussionen geht es heute darum, dass die neuen Kunstmuseen entweder zu ausdrucksstark sind, um einen guten Ausstellungsraum abzugeben, oder ins andere Extrem verfallen: eine Ansammlung weißer Kästen, die der Kunst das Leben aussaugen. Wir wählten einen dritten Weg: Die gesamte Präsentation – alle sieben Tafeln – beschränkte sich auf Schwarz und Weiß.

Skandinavisches Blut / Nordlicht
Mein Großvater wurde in Tønsberg, Norwegen, geboren. Mein Vater, ein echter Norweger, ließ uns am Rand der Meerenge Puget Sound, nahe Seattle, aufwachsen. Der niedrige Einfall des nördlichen Sonnenlichtes im Winter hat hier eine besondere, inspirierende Kraft – ähnlich wie in Skandinavien. Im Jahr 1993 wurden wir aufgefordert, an dem Wettbewerb für das Museum of Contemporary Art in Helsinki teilzunehmen. Das Konzept in unserem Entwurf »Kiasma«, das nördliche Licht mit der Struktur und Landschaft der Stadt zu verflechten, war erfolgreich, und unser Projekt wurde aus 516 Beiträgen ausgewählt. Die Aufmerksamkeit auf den niedrigen Lichteinfall in Helsinki wurde in einem »Lichtfang«-Abschnitt entwickelt.

Gegenwärtig arbeiten wir an der Fertigstellung des Knut Hamsun Centers oberhalb des Polarkreises in Hamarøy, Norwegen. Hier ist der nördliche Charakter des Lichtes extrem: Es gibt sechs Nächte im Sommer, in denen um Mitternacht die Sonne scheint, und im Januar gibt es überhaupt keine Sonne.

Diese Bauerfahrungen und mein skandinavisches Blut haben mir beim Plan, das Gebäude in Herning mit einer bestimmten Lichtqualität an seinen Standort zu binden, einen gewissen Vorsprung gegeben. Die geschwungenen, flachen, »ärmelartigen« Dächer biegen sich mit Oberlichtstreifen auf, um den flachen Winkel des Sonnenlichts einzufangen, damit es sanft über die geschwungene Decke hinwegfällt. Die Geometrie der Licht reflektierenden Wellen verteilt das Licht so wunderbar in den Ausstellungsräumen, dass sie ohne künstliche Beleuchtung genutzt werden können. Der Raum wird belebt und ist lebendig, wenn sich eine Wolke vor die Sonne schiebt oder von der Sonne wegzieht, wie es in dieser Region häufig geschieht.

Flächige Architektur / Textile Formen
Dem flachen Charakter der geschwungenen Dachelemente, die die Schatzkästchen der Galerie bedecken, folgte die flächige Entwicklung der anderen Räume in weißem Beton. Fahrzeugplanen wurden in die Betonschalung eingelassen, um die Struktur von Textilien nachzuahmen, die die

Unvollkommenheiten der schnellen Konstruktion überdeckt. Böden aus vollständig kohlefarbenem Beton lassen den Grundriss zu einer durchlaufenden Patina mit einer gewachsten Oberfläche verschmelzen. Indirektes Licht an Orten wie dem Café wurde durch sandgestrahltes Glas erreicht. Erdhügel, die die Geometrie des Gebäudes in der Landschaft weiterführen, schaffen um das Gebäude herum Räume. Beim Eingang formt der geschwungene Hügel einen Raum, der vor der danebenliegenden Autobahn schützt.

Auf der Südseite sammeln und reflektieren große, spiegelnde Bassins das Sonnenlicht auf die Gewölbedecken. Der Landschaftsarchitekt Torben Schønherr hat unser Wettbewerbskonzept mit seiner eigenen feinen, lockeren Pflasterung und Bepflanzung weiterentwickelt.

Ein Anruf an Halloween

Nachdem wir gerade noch den Abgabetermin zum Einsenden der Tafeln eingehalten hatten, wendeten wir uns einem anderen Projekt zu und vergaßen den Wettbewerb. Dann, am 31. Oktober – an Halloween –, bekam ich einen Anruf von Holger Reenberg, dem Direktor: »Steven, Du hast den Wettbewerb gewonnen! Wir wollen das [Museum] innerhalb von zwei Jahren bauen und dort einziehen!« Aus Kopenhagen kommend, konnte der Anrufer natürlich nicht wissen, was es in New York bedeutete, davon an Halloween benachrichtigt zu werden: einem Tag der Angst, gemischt mit Freude.

Realisierung: Lichtraum der Überraschung

Das Buch *Questions of Perception,* das ich gemeinsam mit Juhani Pallasmaa und Alberto Pérez-Gómez 1994 schrieb, enthält das Kapitel, »Perspective Space. Incomplete Perception« (»Perspektivischer Raum. Unvollständige Wahrnehmung«). Darin argumentieren wir, dass sich unsere Wahrnehmung von Raum aus einer Reihe von sich überlappenden Perspektiven entwickelt, die sich entsprechend dem Blickwinkel von Geschwindigkeit und Bewegung entfalten. Während wir vielleicht unsere Bewegung entlang eines genauen Weges bei einer bestimmten Geschwindigkeit analysieren, können wir niemals alle möglichen Ansichten aufzählen.

Das Gebäude in Herning ist eine physische Umsetzung dieser Ideen. Anstatt ein Gebäude zu sein, das man zunächst als ein Objekt wahrnimmt, weist es eine Reihe von Außenerfahrungen auf, die mit der Landschaft verschmolzen sind. Während man um das Gebäude herumgeht, erlebt man sehr unterschiedliche Räume, die sich jeweils nicht zu einem Objekt oder einer Singularität addieren lassen. In das Gebäude hineinzugehen ist eine ganz andere Erfahrung. Man ist irgendwie überrascht, wenn man es betritt, vor allem wenn man am Ende des Tages, gegen 17:30 Uhr, ankommt, wenn der niedrige Einfallswinkel der westlichen Sonne durch die zwei tief geschwungen Wellen zu wehen scheint und sich das Licht an der Decke sammelt.

Wenn man sich durch die schräg stehenden, gerade verlaufenden Wände bewegt, die die Galerie einfassen, gleitet der Raum vom einen zum anderen hinüber, wo die strahlende Kurve der Decke einer Fließrichtung durch eine Reihe von Räumen folgt. Die Ausstellungsräume, in denen die Wände immer im rechten Winkel zu den Böden stehen, sind so geformt, dass der Schwerpunkt auf der Kunst liegt, während weiter außen die Kanten undeutlicher werden und mit der Landschaft in Beziehung treten. Die Räumlichkeiten des Cafés dehnen sich bis auf die Terrasse aus. Die Konzerthalle für das MidWest Ensemble öffnet sich zu seinen eigenen Probe- und Betriebsräumen hin, während es an die zentrale Eingangshalle anschließt. Die Ausstellungsräume im Zentrum des Gebäudes können leicht geschlossen werden, auch wenn alle sie umgebenden Räume während dieser Schließzeiten offen bleiben und genutzt werden können. Der monochrome Rahmen stellt die Farbe der Kunst, die den Raum, je nach Künstler und Ausstellung, unterschiedlich mit Spannung auflädt, in den Vordergrund. Die rechtwinkligen Räume der Galerie sind ganz genau im Verhältnis von 1:1,618 gebaut, so wie wir das bei allen unseren Projekten machen. In seinem wichtigen Buch *The Geometry of Art and Life* (»Die Geometrie von Kunst und Leben«, 1946) argumentiert Matila Ghyka für Proportionen, die auf mathematischen Prinzipien beruhen, die man in der Natur findet; das Verhältnis des goldenen Schnittes, 1:1,618, ist das Schlüsselverhältnis bei organischem Wachstum.

Während man durch die Räume läuft, die zu den Büroräumen führen, lädt das Vorhandensein des geschwungenen Flachdachs den Raum wieder energetisch auf – allerdings in einer sich nach oben bewegenden Kurve, die zur außen liegenden Landschaft leitet. Bei den täglichen Aufgaben all derer, die in dem Museum arbeiten, wird die flächige und Licht einfangende Geometrie der Architektur die Aktivitäten innen und nach außen in die Landschaft hinein beleben. Der monochrome Rahmen der Museumsarchitektur wird vom Wechsel der Lichteinfälle tagtäglich und in den verschiedenen Jahreszeiten belebt. Mit seiner Konzerthalle, die auch als Veranstaltungsbühne dienen kann, seiner pädagogischen Abteilung für Kinder und Erwachsene, dem Restaurant und den Versammlungsorten unter freiem Himmel besteht die Hoffnung, dass das Museum als eine Art sozialer Kondensator für die Gemeinde fungieren wird. Der Kern des Museums – die Galerien – will ein Lichtraum für wechselnde Kunstausstellungen sein.

Als er sie zum ersten Mal sah, sagte der Künstler Jannis Kounellis, dass ihn die Räume an Schuppen mit herabhängenden Fischernetzen erinnern. Vielleicht kann man hier in der weitläufigen, flachen Gegend von Jütland ein bisschen vom Meer fühlen. Ein Anschwellen der Landschaft, die sich in Lichtwellen verwandelt, um einen Nullpunkt zu erreichen, von dem aus, wie Piero Manzoni sagte, »alles möglich ist«.

idee und phänomen

Juhani Pallasmaa

»Architekturtheorie bedeutet das Überdenken von Phänomenen, die ihren Anfang in Ideen haben. Indem wir etwas ›erschaffen‹, realisieren wir, dass die Idee nur die Saat ist, die in Phänomenen aufgeht.«
Steven Holl, *Anchoring*

Steven Holls Entwicklung als Architekt – von den frühen Projekten seit Mitte der 1970er-Jahre, in denen sich die Ideen des zeitgenössischen italienischen Rationalismus widerspiegeln, bis hin zum gelassenen und experimentell vielschichtigen HEART Herning Museum of Contemporary Art, das in diesem Jahr eröffnet wird – ist lang und voller Überraschungen. Die fünfundzwanzig Jahre, die diese entgegengesetzten Phasen seiner Karriere trennen, scheinen mehr als ein ganzes Leben voller intensiver Erforschung von Form, Wahrnehmung und vom Geist der Baukunst verschmelzen zu lassen. Seine Reise als Designer wurde durch die unablässige Lektüre von Poesie (darunter Dichter wie Osip Mandelstam, Anna Achmatowa und Paul Celan, zusätzlich zu Dichtern, die auf Englisch schreiben), von philosophischen Werken und von wissenschaftlicher Literatur sowie einer intensiven Auseinandersetzung mit der Welt der bildenden Künste geleitet. Die Bandbreite seiner Entwürfe ist außergewöhnlich abwechslungsreich und dabei gleichzeitig unbeirrt und beständig, als ob sie einem vorgefassten Plan gefolgt wäre. Während sich dieser Weg geschlängelt und in neue Richtungen verzweigt hat, hat er auch, allmählich und überzeugend, die einzigartige, unverkennbare Welt des Architekten Steven Holl erschaffen. Die jüngste Verleihung des Frontiers of Knowledge Awards in the Arts durch die spanische BBVA-Stiftung bestätigt, dass er einer der international angesehensten Architekten ist. Zweifellos war er während der letzen zwei Jahrzehnte auch eines der weltweit inspirierendsten Beispiele und Vorbilder in Bezug auf das Unterrichten von Architektur. Seine Offenheit und seine Neugierde wie auch die seltene Fähigkeit, kreatives Design mit philosophischer Klarheit und poetischem Ausdruck zu verschmelzen, haben seinen Einfluss in der Welt der Architekturpädagogik weiter verstärkt.

Die künstlerischen Universen von Architekten und Künstlern neigen dazu, im Laufe der Zeit und in der Folge einer bewussten Suche nach einer wiedererkennbaren künstlerischen Identität immer spezifischer, enger und hermetischer zu werden. Holls Welt hat sich immer wieder neuen Einflüssen, Bestrebungen und architektonischen Lösungen geöffnet. Seine Gebäude sind keine Variationen einer etablierten Architekturanatomie oder seiner früheren Architekturthemen; eher sind es neue architektonische Typologien, Anatomien und räumliche Erfahrungen. Sein frühes Interesse an architektonischen Typologien hat sich später in seinem fortgesetzten Streben danach, neue Architekturtypen hervorzubringen, quasi neue Architekturwesen zu schaffen, widergespiegelt. Er scheint jedem neuen Auftrag sozusagen eine neuartige Architektur-DNA zu injizieren und unvorhersehbare Architekturtypen zu erschaffen. Man denke nur an die dramatischen Unterschiede zwischen, sagen wir mal, dem labyrinthischen Entwurf für den Palazzo del Cinema in Venedig (1990), der ein wenig an die Falten des menschlichen Gehirns erinnert, dem Gesamteindruck von geformtem, moduliertem Licht in der St.-Ignatius-Kapelle an der Seattle University (1994–1997), der gigantischen, porösen urbanen Wand und den gebauten Höhlen des Studentenwohnheims Simmons Hall am Massachusetts Institute of Technology in Cambridge (1992–2002), der silbrig fließenden zusammensetzbaren Form der Whitney Water Purification Facility mit angrenzendem Park in Connecticut (1998–2005), die Assoziationen der Leben spendenden Reinheit des Wassers hervorruft, und der beleuchteten Glasbalken–Laternen oder »Linsen« des Nelson-Atkins Museum of Art in Kansas City (1999–2007), die gebieterisch vom Boden aufsteigen. Ungeachtet seines Interesses an integrierten und gestalteten Räumen und Formen erschafft er gelegentlich Projekte, die auf einer strengen, rechtwinkligen Geometrie und einer einfachen tektonischen Sprache beruhen, wie die Swiss Residence in Washington D. C. (2001–2006), das Writing With Light House auf Long Island (2001–2004) und das Planar House in Paradise Valley, Arizona (2002–2005).

Wie bei allen Architekten standen am Anfang von Holls Karriere kleine, theoretische Projekte wie die Innenausstattung von Geschäftsräumen, Renovierungen und Häuser, aber mittlerweile leitet er urbane Projekte von enormer Größe wie das Makuhari-Housing-Projekt in Chiba, Japan (1992–1996), den multifunktionalen Häuserblock Linked Hybrid in Peking mit über 2500 Bewohnern (2003–2008), und den Wettbewerbsbeitrag für das World Trade Center in New York (2002).[1] Bei seinen neuesten Projekten hat sich der Architekt außerdem ernsthaft mit ökologischen Lösungen wie beispielsweise dem Heizen und Kühlen durch Erdwärme und dem Recycling von Wasser beschäftigt. Die unermüdliche Neugierde und die mentale Energie, welche die meisten von Holls Projekten ausstrahlen, lassen mich vermuten, dass ihn seine Expeditionen auch in Zukunft zu bislang unbekannten Territorien führen werden.

Bereits in den frühen 1980er-Jahren hatte ich die wenigen publizierten Projekte von Steven Holl wie den äußerst strategischen Manila-Housing-Competition-Plan (1975), das teilweise unter Wasser gelegene Sokol Retreat in Saint-Tropez, (1976), die Bronx Gymnasium Bridge, New York (1977), die Bridge of Houses on Elevated Rail, New York (1980–1982) und das Autonomous-Artisans'-Housing-Projekt, Staten Island (1980–1984), aufmerksam verfolgt. Mich faszinierte die Kombination des streng Rationalen mit dem Surrealen

oder der fantastischen Natur dieser Architekturentwürfe ebenso wie die poetische Präzision seiner minimalistischen Strichzeichnungen, die den zeitgenössischen, elegant schlichten Zeichnungen von Mark Mack ähnelten. Das Gefühl der Lebensnähe, das durch Möbel und Alltagsgegenstände hervorgerufen wurde, erinnerte mich an die reduzierten, perspektivischen Zeichnungen von Heinrich Tessenow, welche die gemütliche Atmosphäre des häuslichen Lebens ausstrahlen. In den 1980er-Jahren hatte ich auch die Fotos einiger Häuser, die Holl gebaut hatte, in Architekturzeitschriften gesehen: das Pool House und Sculpture Studio in Scarsdale, New York (1980), das Haus auf Martha's Vineyard, Massachusetts (1984–1988), und das Hybrid Building in Seaside, Florida (1984–1988), die alle eine ähnliche, persönliche und konzentrierte Architekturintention zum Ausdruck bringen.

Holls erfolgreicher Wettbewerbsbeitrag für die Amerika-Gedenkbibliothek in Berlin (1988) mit ihrem unorthodoxen, volumetrischen Aufbau und dem seltsam anschwellenden Brückenelement postulierte eine urbane Architektur jenseits sowohl der modernen als auch der postmodernen Bildsprache der Zeit. Die Perspektiven des Innenraums mit den verschiedenen, abgestuften Böden, die in den Raum vorstoßen und sich wieder zurückziehen, erinnerten mich an die unendlichen Labyrinthe von Räumen und Treppen in Giovanni Battista Piranesis hypnotischen *Carceri*-Zeichnungen. Ich erinnere mich daran, dass ich, als ich Anfang der 1960er-Jahre die ersten veröffentlichten Fotos der gotischen Türme von Louis Kahns Richards Medical Research Building in Philadelphia gesehen habe, die gleiche Assoziation hatte. Ich hatte ein ähnliches Schwindelgefühl, als mir klar wurde, dass ich gerade eine neue Architekturwelt betrachtete, deren Pforten eben erst geöffnet worden waren.

Holls interessante und genaue Studie *American Vernacular Typologies* (1982) und auch seine Schriften, die seit dem Ende der 1970er-Jahre in den Publikationen von *Pamphlet Architecture,* die er selbst herausgibt, erscheinen, überzeugten mich schließlich, dass ich es hier mit einem Architekten zu tun hatte, der tatsächlich danach strebt, seine Bauwerke auf den fundierten theoretischen und historischen Grundlagen der Architektur aufzubauen, und dass er deshalb höchstwahrscheinlich in der Lage sein würde, den Horizont zeitgenössischer Architektur zu erweitern, der zwischen einer manieristischen Moderne und einer schmerzhaft eklektischen, postmodernen Bildsprache gefangen zu sein schien.

Originale Entwürfe von Steven Holl sah ich zum ersten Mal 1989 in der Ausstellung seiner Arbeiten im Museum of Modern Art in New York.[2] Vor allem die eleganten Materialkonstruktionen in der Ausstellung, die aus geschwärztem Stahl, Bronze und satiniertem Glas gefertigt waren, zeigten mir, dass es sich um eine sinnliche Architektur handelt, welche die Vorstellungskraft und den Tastsinn anspricht. Diese Konstruktionen schienen sogar andere Sinnesebenen zu sensibilisieren, und mir wurde klar, dass mein ureigenstes Wesen, mein innerstes Verständnis meiner selbst, angesprochen und aktiviert wurde. Holls Ausstellungsarchitektur erinnerte mich an frühere New Yorker Projekte: das Cohen Apartment (1982/83), das Kurtz Apartment (1985), den Pace Collection Showroom (1986) und den Giada Shop (1987), die ein Gefühl des abstrahierten, rhythmischen und geometrischen Raums des Neoplastizismus von De Stijl in Verbindung mit einer Gesamtheit des Raums in sinnlicher Materialität und haptischer Ausdrucksstärke vermitteln. Mir war klar, dass der Architekt inzwischen vollständig seine persönliche künstlerische Welt und ihren Ausdruck gefunden hatte.

Während ich mir die Ausstellung ansah, ahnte ich nicht, dass ich Steven eines Tages – und sogar bald – kennenlernen würde, dass wir gute Freunde werden und manchmal sogar zusammenarbeiten würden.

Im August 1991, mitten in den intensiven, intellektuellen Diskussionen beim fünften Alvar-Aalto-Symposium in Jyväskylä in Finnland, konnte ich Steven überzeugen, sich die außergewöhnliche Petäjävesi-Kirche anzusehen, die etwa vierzig Kilometer entfernt liegt und die 1764 von einem der einheimischen Baumeister erbaut worden war. Auf dem Weg zur Kirche erzählte ich Steven, dass die einfache Zeichnung eines kreuzförmigen Grundrisses für die Kirche, die die lokale Bauernversammlung dem schwedischen Königshof (Finnland gehörte damals zu Schweden) zur Abnahme eingereicht hatte, abgelehnt und dass ein »inakzeptabel« auf den Entwurf gestempelt worden war. Da die Kommunikation zu dieser Zeit allerdings sehr langsam vonstatten ging, hatten die Dorfbewohner bereits mit dem Kirchenbau begonnen, als der Brief mit der Ablehnung aus Stockholm in dem Dorf ankam. Inzwischen ist diese einfache Kirche als Baudenkmal Teil des UNESCO-Weltkulturerbes. Die anrührend ernsthaften Holzgewölbe, die steinerne Renaissancebauten imitierten, besiegelten, glaube ich, unsere Freundschaft.

Bis 1992 hatte Holl relativ kleine Privathäuser gebaut und die Innenausstattung von Geschäftsräumen geplant, und dann bekam er den Auftrag für den Bau des Kiasma Museum of Contemporary Art mitten in Helsinki (1992–1998). Sein Entwurf war aus einem internationalen Wettbewerb mit der Rekordzahl von fünfhundertzwanzig Beiträgen als Sieger hervorgegangen. Auch nach dieser nicht zu leugnenden Autorität, die ihm der Sieg dieses Wettbewerbs verlieh, war die gestalterische Aufgabe kontextuell, funktional, technisch und sogar politisch gesehen außergewöhnlich anspruchsvoll. Jenseits der üblichen Überlegungen in Bezug auf die Architektur musste Holl sich mit der überlebensgroßen Figur von Marschall Mannerheim vertraut machen, dessen Reiterstandbild neben dem Museum eine öffentliche, kontroverse Diskussion über die Eignung von Holls Museum in dieser Lage hervorrief, die das Projekt beinahe verhindert hätte. Dieses Museumsprojekt konfrontierte Holls Architekturbüro mit neuen beruflichen Schwierigkeiten und Anforderungen.

Zeitgleich mit dem Kiasma-Projekt arbeiteten Holl und sein Büro an zwei weiteren, ebenso anspruchsvollen Projekten: dem Cranbrook Institute of Science in Bloomfield Hills,

Michigan (1993–1998), dem Anbau und der Instandsetzung des Museums, das Eliel Saarinen 1931 entworfen hatte (zufälligerweise liegt Kiasma nur einen Gebäudeblock von Eliel Saarinens großem Bahnhof in Helsinki entfernt), und der St.-Ignatius-Kapelle in Seattle, der Stadt, in der Holl seine Kindheit und Jugend verbracht hatte. Diese drei Projekte etablierten Steven Holls Position als einer der innovativsten und profiliertesten Architekten unserer Zeit. Mit diesen parallelen Projekten entwickelte er sein charakteristisches Gefühl für Gesamträume, die über die Idee vom additiven Anordnen hinausgehen, und für seinen typischen Einsatz von indirektem Licht und Farbe, sinnlichen Materialien und haptischer Detailarbeit. Außerdem perfektionierte er seine persönliche Designmethodik und seine Art, mit vielen Assistenten und beratenden Experten zusammenzuarbeiten. Schnell wurde aus seinem Büro ein internationales Unternehmen mit zahlreichen erfolgreichen Wettbewerben und Aufträgen in mehreren europäischen Ländern, im Nahen Osten, Japan, China, Korea und Kambodscha sowie in verschiedenen Städten der Vereinigten Staaten.

Holl hat die Idee nie gefallen, ein rationalisiertes und instrumentalisiertes Büro zu leiten: »Firmenarchitektur« ist ein Begriff, der in seiner Sprache einen höchst negativen Beigeschmack hat. Anstatt linear sich baukastenartig wiederholende und additive Ideen einzusetzen, bemüht er sich um Besonderheiten in der Architektur, und seine Gebäude sehen oft so aus, als seien sie geschnitzt oder gegossen und nicht aus Einzelteilen zusammengesetzte Konstruktionen. Durch diese Eigenschaften entsteht sowohl in den Einzelheiten als auch in der Gesamtheit der Eindruck von Endgültigkeit und Einzigartigkeit. Seine Oberflächengestaltung – wie Fenster und Unterteilungen der Wände oder sogar die Anordnung einer Reihe von Einbauschränken und Schubladen – formen zumeist ineinandergreifende Figuren, die einen optischen Zusammenhalt entstehen lassen, der an die visuelle Einzigartigkeit von Eduardo Chillidas Skulpturen erinnert. Holls Verwendung des goldenen Schnitts als proportionales System unterstützt diesen Eindruck des Zusammenhalts. »Proportionen können eher gefühlt als direkt wahrgenommen werden. Wie die Kakofonie und die Harmonie in der Musik sind sie ziemlich subjektiv und ausdrucksstark«, erklärte er.[3]

Holls entschiedenes und unablässiges Experimentieren und sein ausdrückliches Vermeiden eines festgelegten, wiederkennbaren Stils, werden durch seine Art zu Arbeiten ermöglicht. Er kombiniert eine feine, künstlerische, intime und persönliche Suche durch kleine Skizzen in Wasserfarben mit der Verwendung von poetischen, verbalen Metaphern und starken konzeptionellen Diagrammen (die oft auf wissenschaftlichen Ideen basieren) mit Untersuchungen anhand von Architekturmodellen und, schließlich, mit computergenerierten Entwicklungs- und Herstellungszeichnungen. Der Computer wird eingesetzt, um den Plan zu entwickeln und präzise Unterlagen für die Ausführung zu erstellen, und nicht, um eine formale Sprache oder einen Ausdruck hervorzubringen. »Wir verwenden Computertechnologien in nahezu jedem Stadium des Designprozesses bis auf die erste Konzeption. Für mich muss der erste Entwurf eines Konzepts mit einem analogen Prozess beginnen, der Verstand, Hand und Auge aufs Engste miteinander verbindet. Ich glaube, dass man nur so ganz in Verbindung mit den Feinheiten und Qualitäten der Rolle, die die Intuition für den Entwurf spielt, stehen kann. In der ersten Zeichnung spüre ich eine direkte Verbindung zur intellektuellen Bedeutung und spüre das Verschmelzen des Idee-Raum-Konzepts. Im Anschluss kann die Arbeit dann digital aufgeladen werden. Der Prozess kann unter Verwendung aller möglichen, schnellen Computerhilfsmittel begonnen werden [...]. Positiv gesehen hat das neue Potenzial der Computer unseren Designprozess befreit, um ihn noch einfallsreicher zu machen.«[4]

Die physische und mentale Intimität und Fühlbarkeit der frühen Arbeitsphasen in Verbindung mit dem phänomenologischen Interesse des Architekten an Licht, Materialität und Detailarbeit sichern das Vorhandensein der menschlichen Hand in der Begegnung mit dem vollendeten Gebäude. Holls Gebäude zeigen normalerweise – anstelle der üblichen glatten Perfektion der heutigen Avantgarde und minimalistischen Architekturen – bewusst eine gewisse Grobheit auf. Dieses bewusste Vermeiden erzwungener Perfektion der Oberflächen und Abschlüsse lässt den Eindruck von Offenheit entstehen und stellt eine Einladung dar, anstatt ein Ausschließen und Ablehnen zu vermitteln, wie es obsessiv technisch perfekte Gebäude oft tun.

Steven Holl hat es geschafft, ein außergewöhnlich überzeugendes Zusammenspiel von Idee und Form, Denken und Tun, Worten und Materialien sowie Technologien und künstlerischem Ausdruck zu entwickeln. Die verbalen philosophischen Äußerungen von Architekten widersprechen oftmals den Charakteristika ihrer Entwurfsarbeiten, aber Holls physische Formen und seine Schriften sind aus einem emotionalen und materiellen Fluss, und beide basieren auf der Verbindung von Wahrnehmung, Idee und Gefühl. Sie sind nicht das Produkt theoretischer Spekulation und Verstand, sondern von Vorstellung und gelebter Erfahrung. In seinem ersten Buch, *Anchoring* (1989), bestätigt Holl bereits diese grundlegende Dialektik des Entwurfs, allerdings mit einem Anflug von Zögern: »Die Beziehung des Schreibens zur Architektur bietet nur einen unsicheren Spiegel, den man Beweisen entgegenhält; in einer wortlosen Stille haben wir eine bessere Chance, in den Bereich zu stolpern, der aus Raum, Licht und Materie besteht, der Architektur ist. Auch wenn sie die Architektur nicht vollständig erfassen können, sind Worte doch ein Versprechen. Die Arbeit muss weiterführen, wenn es die Worte allein nicht vermögen. Worte sind Pfeile, die in die richtige Richtung weisen; wenn man sie zusammennimmt, bilden sie eine Landkarte der Intentionen der Architektur.«[5]

Etwa ein Jahrzehnt später sieht er die Rolle der philosophischen Untersuchung relativ klar und eindeutig: »Eine Architekturphilosophie, mag sie noch so locker sein, leitet die Arbeit eines jeden denkenden Architekten. Es ist für mich ein immer noch anhaltendes, lebenslanges Projekt – parallel zu meinen Gebäuden –, einen schriftlichen Bericht über den Anspruch der Architektur, eine Form von Idee zu sein, zu verfassen. Von meinem ersten kleinen Manifest *Anchoring* (1989) bis hin zu unserer Gemeinschaftsarbeit *Questions of Perception* (1994) ist eine Philosophie der Architektur das schwer fassbare und nie erreichte Ziel. Die Freude, Konstruktionen zu erbauen, die auf größeren Ideen beruhen, ist ein wundervolles Geheimnis.«[6]

Holl begann früh, verbale und literarische Konzepte als inspirierende und leitende geistige Bilder in seinem Designprozess zu verwenden. Herman Melvilles *Moby Dick* war die Inspiration für das Berkowitz House auf Martha's Vineyard in Massachusetts (1984) oder, genauer gesagt, es war die Geschichte, der zufolge die Indianer des Stammes, der ursprünglich in dieser Gegend lebte, eine einzigartige Form von Unterkunft schufen, indem sie Häute oder Rinden über das Skelett eines Wales spannten, das sie am Strand gefunden hatten. Holls Haus am Strand ist ein metaphorisches Skelett mit einem dichten Holzrahmen, der für die Rippen des Wales steht.

Holl gab den unterschiedlichen Einheiten des Bridge-of-Houses-Projekts Namen, um anzudeuten, dass hier unterschiedliche Bewohner lebten, für die es wiederum unterschiedliche Architekturgeschichten gab, die auf die individuellen Bewohner zugeschnitten waren: Haus des Bestimmers, Haus des Zweiflers, Haus für einen Mann ohne Meinung, Das Rätsel, Traumhaus, Vier-Turm-Haus, Materie und Gedächtnis. Die fiktiven Kunden, die er sich für das Projekt des Autonomous Artisans' Housing ausdachte, waren: Papierhersteller, Holzarbeiter, Bootbauer, Steinmetz, Glasradierer, Verputzer, Metallarbeiter. Ähnlich waren auch die fiktiven Kunden der »Gesellschaft der Fremden« des Hybrid Buildings, das er in Florida baute: tragischer Dichter, Musiker und Mathematiker. Die Personifizierung von Bewohnern in einem Wohnungsbauprojekt scheint dabei zu helfen, die befremdliche Leere der Anonymität zu überwinden; ein tiefgründiger Architekt stellt sich das Leben vor, das in dem Raum stattfindet, den er entwirft, und nicht nur seine geometrischen und optischen Eigenschaften. »Stellen wir uns eine Wand vor: Was findet dahinter statt?«, rät uns Architekten der Dichter Jean Tardieu.[7] Und doch sind wir häufig nicht daran interessiert, uns das Leben vorzustellen, das in den Häusern stattfindet, die wir entwerfen.

Holls Entwurf für das Knut Hamsun Center (1994–2009) in Hamarøy, Norwegen, das sich momentan in der Endphase des Baus befindet, ist ein Plan, der von einem literarischen Konzept, von Hamsuns literarischem Meisterwerk *Hunger* (1890), geleitet wird. Das Grundkonzept des »Körpers der unsichtbaren Kräfte« basiert auf dem Geständnis, das der Autor halb im Delirium von sich gibt: »Ich war so vollständig eine Beute unsichtbarer Einflüsse.«[8] Der Architekt hat auch andere Szenen aus dem Roman mit einbezogen wie zum Beispiel »ein Mädchen mit aufgestülpten Ärmeln lehnte sich heraus und begann die Scheiben auf der Außenseite zu putzen«.[9]

Holl hat in seiner Architektur auch musikalische Metaphern oder Analogien verwendet. Das Stretto House in Dallas,

Texas (1989–1991) basiert auf dem musikalischen Konzept des »stretto« (ein Fugenmotiv, das verwendet wird, um sich selbst zu begleiten und einen Kontrapunkt zu bilden) und Béla Bartóks *Musik für Saiteninstrumente, Schlagzeug und Celesta* (1937). Die vier Sätze der Partitur sowie auch ihre Unterteilung in einzelne Komponenten wie Schlagzeug (schwer) und Saiteninstrument (leicht), spiegeln sich in der räumlichen, formalen und materiellen Struktur des Hauses. Ein weiteres Beispiel einer Inspiration durch die Musik für Holls Werk ist sein Projekt für die Sarphatistraat Offices in Amsterdam (1996–2000): Gespiegeltes Licht und Farbe, gefangen hinter der perforierten Metallfassade, erinnern an ein Konzept, das auf der Musik von Morton Feldmans *Patterns in a Chromatic Field* basiert.

Steven Holls effizientestes kreatives Werkzeug ist das Konzept, eine kraftvolle Verschmelzung einer Metapher und einer Architekturidee in einem einzigen Leitbild. Seine metaphorischen Designkonzepte wie Sieben Flaschen Licht in einer Steinschachtel (St.-Ignatius-Kapelle), Seltsame Attraktoren, Haus aus Dampf, Geschichte des Wassers, Garten der Wissenschaft und Haus aus Eis (Anbau des Cranbrook Institute of Science), Dreifachheit und Regel der rechten Hand (Bellevue Art Museum, 1997–2001), Menger-Schwamm (Sarphatistraat Offices), Porosität (Simmons Hall, 1999–2002), Stein und Feder (Nelson-Atkins Museum of Art, 1999–2007) und Schreiben mit Licht (Long Island, 2001–2004) verweisen alle auf Bilder aus Poesie oder Wissenschaft. Maurice Merleau-Pontys Begriff »Chiasmus«, den der Architekt als das Leitkonzept und auch als Decknamen für seinen Wettbewerbsbeitrag für das Museum of Contemporary Art in Helsinki verwendet hat, wurde später sogar als Name für das Museum angenommen: Kiasma.[10]

Seit Beginn seiner Karriere hat Holl sich mit der Strategie des »eingeschränkten Konzepts« auseinandergesetzt, die, wie er schreibt, »für jedes Baugelände und jeden einzigartigen Entwurf umformuliert wird. [...] Sprache wird zum Vehikel der ›Wiedererkennung des Konzepts‹ wie Ernst Cassirer in seinem Buch *Philosophie der symbolischen Formen* (1923–1929) ausführlich erklärt.«[11] Holl erläutert die wichtige Rolle der konzeptionellen Diagramme in seinem Entwurfsprozess: »Ich bin vollkommen abhängig von Konzeptdiagrammen. Sie sind meine Geheimwaffe, mit denen ich mich mit frischem Wind von einem Projekt zum nächsten, und von einem Bauort zum nächsten bewegen kann. Wenn ich meine Projekte mit einem fixen Formenvokabular angehen würde, wäre ich jetzt erschöpft und hätte das Interesse für Architektur schon lange verloren. Ein Anfangskonzept für jedes Projekt zu finden, das auf die Essenz und die einzigartigen architektonischen Möglichkeiten des Ortes eingeht, ist für mich ein Weg, in die Arbeit zu kommen. Es ist mein Tor zu neuen architektonischen Ideen. Obwohl die meisten LiebhaberInnen meiner Arbeit ihre Erfahrungs- und phänomenologischen Qualitäten wie z. B. das Licht oder die verwendeten Materialien schätzen, ist für mich die Idee das wichtigste.«[12]

Im Rahmen eines Gesprächs, das wir 2002 für die spanische Zeitschrift *El Croquis* führten, bewertete Holl seine Arbeitsmethode wie folgt: »Ein Konzept ist der ›Motor‹, der den Designprozess antreibt. Am Anfang jeden Projektes, nachdem wir das Baugelände und den Plan analysiert haben, und manchmal nach einigen Fehlstarts, entschließen wir uns für ein Grundkonzept (oder –konzepte) und erstellen erste räumliche Skizzen. Weil die Bedingungen bei jedem Baugelände einzigartig sind, bemühen wir uns um gleichermaßen ausgewogene und spezifische Lösungen. Das Konzept, das in Worten und Diagrammen zum Ausdruck kommt, hilft uns, die unterschiedlichsten Aspekte zu vereinen. Es fördert die Entwicklung eines Projektes und die Kommunikation mit dem Kunden [...]. In gewisser Weise sind die individuellen ›poetischen Ideen‹ nicht nur die Motoren, die den Entwurf antreiben – sie sind die großen Befreier, die eine Verbindung zu der größeren Gedankenwelt anderer Disziplinen herstellen.«[13]

Holls außergewöhnliche Offenheit und seine Aufnahmebereitschaft im Entwurfsprozess werden durch kritische Diskussionen über aktuelle Projekte in seinem Büro, zu denen er neben seinen Angestellten oft auch Kritiker von außen einlädt, verdeutlicht. Während der Design- und Entwicklungsphase des Kiasma-Museums in Helsinki war ich oft überrascht, dass er willens und in der Lage war, Vorschläge oder Anforderungen des Kunden zu akzeptieren, auch wenn sie manchmal unangemessen waren oder im Widerspruch zu den ursprünglichen Absichten des Architekten standen. Er schaffte es, diese Begebenheiten in positive Impulse innerhalb des Entwicklungsprozesses umzuwandeln, anstatt sie als unwillkommene Störungen oder Kompromisse zu betrachten.

Ungeachtet seines Engagements für einen konzeptgeleiteten Entwurfsprozess ist Steven Holl einer der wichtigsten Vertreter des phänomenologischen Ansatzes in der heutigen Architekturszene. Seit seinen frühen Schriften und Entwürfen hat er sich auf die experimentellen und phänomenologischen Dimensionen der Architektur konzentriert, die sich in der Begegnung mit der Arbeit an sich ergeben. Anstelle der formalistischen Betrachtungen, die heutzutage in der Architekturtheorie beliebt sind, untersucht er die Wahrnehmungsphänomene, die implizit in den verschiedenen Aspekten des Projekts zu finden sind, und er strebt nach echten Erfahrungen der Sinne und des Geistes und vor allem nach haptischen Qualitäten, nach »der haptischen Welt«. Seine ersten Versuche mit Aquarellskizzen wie auch die spätere Weiterentwicklung in Architekturmodellen verstärken die Präsenz der materiellen und experimentellen Realität. Holl erläutert die phänomenologische Grundlage seiner Arbeit folgendermaßen: »In der Architektur verflechten sich die Wahrnehmungen von Zeit, Raum, Licht und Materialien, die auf einem ›vortheoretischen Grund‹ existieren. Die Phänomena, die innerhalb eines Raums vorkommen, wie zum Beispiel das Licht, das durch ein Fenster eindringt, oder die Farbe oder Reflexion eines Materials auf einer Oberfläche, haben alle im Bereich der Wahrnehmung entscheidende Beziehungen. Die Transparenz einer

Folie, die kreidige Stumpfheit von Gips, die glänzende Reflexion von Milchglas und der Sonnenstrahl verbinden sich alle in wechselseitigen Beziehungen, die die besondere Atmosphäre eines Ortes ausmachen.«[14]

Angesichts der Tatsachen, dass Steven Holl selbst seit seiner frühen Jugend malt, heute mit Künstlern zusammenarbeitet und sich leidenschaftlich für Kunst interessiert, überrascht es nicht, dass er zu den Architekten gehört, denen man beim Bau zeitgenössischer Museen am meisten vertraut.[15] Auf seiner Projektliste stehen zurzeit mehr als ein Dutzend Wettbewerbsbeiträge, ausgeführte Kunstmuseen und andere Ausstellungsräume. Darüber hinaus hat er an fast zehn anderen Museumsprojekten mitgewirkt, darunter auch Kino- und Spielzeugmuseen, naturhistorische Museen, Museen über die Evolution des Menschen, Architektur oder die Zivilisation des Mittelmeerraumes.

Der jüngste Museumsentwurf von Steven Holl, HEART, ist das ungezwungene, überzeugte Projekt eines Designers, der Erfahrung im Bauen von Räumen für Kunst hat. Da sich das Gelände gegenüber einer ehemaligen Hemdenfabrik befindet (in der das Museum vorrübergehend untergebracht war), das in der Form eines Hemdkragens erbaut ist, führt Holl die an Claes Oldenburg erinnernde, spielerische Pop-Art-Bildersprache fort, indem er das neue Museum als Hemdsärmel, die sich überkreuzen, entwarf. Die beiden eigentlichen Ausstellungsräume, die »Schatzkästchen«, sind rechteckige Räume, wohingegen sich die anderen Funktionsräume und Einrichtungen um diesen rechteckigen und operativ unabhängigen Kern in einer frei geformten Kontur herum gruppieren. Der Architekt selbst betont seine Absicht, ein Museum als eine Reihe von räumlichen Erfahrungen zu entwerfen, die durch das Zusammenspiel der Teile des Museums und die angrenzenden Böschungen entstehen sollen, anstatt das Museum als ein Objekt zu verstehen. Die Idee der unterschiedlichen Bereiche erschafft einen abwechslungsreichen Rhythmus von abgehängten Segelformen oder diagonalen Wellenmustern, über und unabhängig von der Anordnung des Grundrisses, wodurch sich verändernde Tageslichtbedingungen in den Ausstellungsräumen entstehen.

Da ich noch nie im HEART gewesen bin, muss ich davon Abstand nehmen, die Räume und ihre Eigenschaften weiter zu beschreiben, da die Qualitäten jeder ernsthaften Architektur, die bewusst auf das tatsächliche, physische Erleben abzielt, nur im »Fleisch der Welt« – um einen wichtigen Begriff von Merleau-Ponty, einem der Lieblingsphilosophen von Holl, aufzugreifen – erfahren und beurteilt werden können.[16]

Während des Baus von HEART näherte sich auch ein weiteres Projekt von Steven Holl in Skandinavien, das Knut Hamsun Center in Hamarøy – ganz in der Nähe des Geburtsortes des Schriftstellers, weit jenseits des Polarkreises in Norwegen – nach fünfzehn Jahren Verzögerung schließlich seiner Vollendung. Dieses Projekt, bei dem es um den politisch umstrittenen Schriftsteller Knut Hamsun geht, der 1920 den Nobelpreis für Literatur erhielt, zeigt Holls Vorstellungs-

kraft und seine Fähigkeit zur Empathie. Das Projekt verbindet typisch Norwegisches mit einer surrealen, ruhelosen Bildersprache, die der Aufgabe vollständig entspricht, aber die Stimmung, die an einen Traum erinnert, scheint den Architekten auch wieder auf die leicht unwirklichen Qualitäten seiner frühesten Werke zurückzuführen. Durch leichte Verschiebungen und Verzerrungen (ein sich unmerklich neigender, scheinbar instabiler Turm, auf dessen Dach »Haare« zu wachsen scheinen) evoziert Holl die Stimmung des Mystischen, des Außergewöhnlichen, das durch die Bilder entsteht, die gleichzeitig märchenhaft und vertraut erscheinen. Der schwarze Turm erhebt sich gleichzeitig gemütlich und verstörend über der Mitte der traditionellen, rotbemalten Häuser von Nordnorwegen mit ihren typischen Rasendächern, während die Form des Turmes auch mit den umgebenden Bergen Kontakt aufnimmt. Das Gebäude ist durch Fenster, die ganz oben eingelassen sind, damit das Licht der Sonne, wenn sie an ihrem höchsten Punkt im 47-Grad-Winkel steht, durch den ganzen Turm hindurch bis zum Boden einfallen kann, mit seiner nordischen Umgebung verbunden. Holls Projekt beweist, dass Architektur Geschichten erzählen kann und dass sie die Macht hat, Dinge des Lebens zu poetisieren, scheinbar bedeutungslosen Dingen einen Stellenwert zu verleihen und die Geheimnisse hinter unseren alltäglichen Erfahrungen zu enthüllen.

»Wir […] bemühen uns, die grundlegenden Erfahrungen alltäglicher Phänomene zu erkunden. Alltägliche und ungewöhnliche Tatsachen, Umstände und Erlebnisse, wenn man sie wichtig nimmt, können bedeutungsvolle Architektur hervorbringen.«[17]

Steven Holl Architects / Watercolor / HEART

1   Das Projekt entstand in Zusammenarbeit mit Richard Meier and Partners, Eisenman Architects und Gwathmey Siegel &
    Associates Architects.
2   Ausstellung *Steven Holl / Emilio Ambasz,* The Museum of Modern Art, New York, Februar bis April 1989.
3   Steven Holl und Juhani Pallasmaa, »A conversation with Steven Holl. Thought, Matter and Experience«, in: *El Croquis,* 108,
    2002, S. 24.
4   Ebd., S. 25.
5   Steven Holl, *Anchoring,* New York 1989, S. 9.
6   Holl und Pallasmaa 2002 (wie Anm. 3), S. 12. Holl bezieht sich hier auf Alberto Pérez-Gómez und Juhani Pallasmaa, »Questions of
    Perception: Phenomenology of Architecture«, in: *A + U Special Issue,* Juli 1994.
7   Zit. n. Georges Perec, *Tiloja avaruuksia* [Espèces d'espaces], Helsinki 1992, S. 72.
8   Knut Hamsun, *Hunger,* München 1974, S. 28.
9   Ebd.
10 Maurice Merleau-Ponty beschreibt die Begriffe von Verflechtung und Chiasmus in seinem Aufsatz »The Intertwining. The
    Chiasm«, in: Maurice Merleau-Ponty, *The Visible and the Invisible,* hrsg. von Claude Lefort, Evanston, Illinois 1992, S. 130–155.
11 Holl und Pallasmaa 2002 (wie Anm. 3), S. 12.
12 Steven Holl, *Idee und Phänomen,* Baden 2002, S. 73.
13 Holl und Pallasmaa 2002 (wie Anm. 3), S. 16.
14 Steven Holl, *Arc en rêve centre d'architecture,* Zürich 1994, S. 3.
15 Holls Bruder ist Maler, und Steven selbst begann 1959 mit dem Malen, bevor er anfing, sich für Architektur zu interessieren.
    Bereits im Alter von zwölf Jahren stellte er seine Gemälde auf der Kitsap Country Fair im Staat Washington aus. Holl gibt zu,
    dass seine Begegnungen mit Donald Judd, Dennis Oppenheim, Richard Nonas, Meg Webster, James Turrell und anderen Künstlern
    nach 1976 in New York für die Entwicklung seiner Ideen in der Architektur von großer Bedeutung waren. Holl und Pallasmaa
    2002 (wie Anm. 3), S. 8. In vielen seiner Projekte hat Holl mit bedeutenden Künstlern wie Vito Acconci und Walter de Maria
    zusammengearbeitet.
16 Maurice Merleau-Ponty beschreibt den Begriff des »Fleisches« in seinem Aufsatz »The Intertwining. The Chiasm«,
    in: Merleau-Ponty 1992 (wie Anm. 10).
17 Steven Holl, »Foreword«, in: *Intertwining,* New York 1996, S. 7.

heart project

Clients, contractors, and suppliers
Client: HEART Art Project Foundation
User group: HEART, Herning Museum of Contemporary Art, Ensemble MidtVest , Socle du Monde ApS
Client's advisor: COWI A/S
Architect: Steven Holl Architects
Architect, Denmark: Kjaer & Richter A/S
Landscape architect: Schoenherr Landskab A/S
Engineers: NIRAS A/S
Indoor climate: Transsolar GmbH
Main contractor: C.C. Contractor, Herning

heart the foundation

Board of Governors
Henning Kruse Petersen
Lars Rohde, ATP
Michael Gaarmann, Albihns AB
Torben Nielsen, Danmarks Nationalbank (National Bank of Denmark)
Kenneth Iversen, Unimerco
Fritz Schur Jr. Fritz Schur A/S

Board of Directors
Lars Damgaard, chairman (HEART)
Lars Krarup, deputy chairman (Municipality of Herning)
Ulla Diderichsen (HEART)
Susanne Olufsen (Ensemble MidtVest)
Henning Kruse Petersen, observer (Socle du Monde)
Johannes Poulsen (Municipality of Herning)
Jørgen Krogh, deputy member (Municipality of Herning)
Holger Reenberg, secretary (HEART)

heart support

Public funding
The Danish Ministry of Culture's fund for
the provinces
County of Ringkjøbing
Municipality of Herning
Municipality of Ikast-Brande

Foundations
The Augustinus Foundation
Bonusfonden
The Obel Family Foundation
Dronning Margrethes og Prins Henriks Fond
The Ege Foundation
The Realdania Foundation
The Hans Foxby Foundation
Herning Folkeblads Fond
Johannes Jensen og Helle Mau Jensens Fond
Knud Højgaards Fond
Lokale- & Anlægsfonden
Midtjydsk Skole- og Kulturfond
The Nordea Denmark Foundation
The Oticon Foundation
Spar Nord Fonden
The Tryg Foundation
The Tuborg Foundation

Sponsors / support from
BDO ScanRevision
cc contractor
Claire
Club 8 Company
CO3
Cowi
Dahl
DSB
Ejendomsaktieselskabet Avanti
Handelsbanken/Midtbank
herning shipping a.s.
I.B. & Co
IBF
IBI
KBT Holding
Knud Højgaards Fond
KPC Byg
KPMG
Lee Sign
Martin Pedersen Strømpefabrik
Montana
Mr. Dohm
Niebuhr Tandhjulsfabrik
Nordea
Nykredit
Nyt Syn
Partner Herning
Partner Revision
Ringkjøbing Amt
Ringkøbing Landbobank
Sanita
Sejerkilde
Spar Nord Bank
Sydbank
Søren Thygesen
Thygesen Textile Group
Aage Damgaard ApS

Editor: Holger Reenberg
Copyediting: Lene Elsner (Danish); Birte Kreft, Hatje Cantz (German); Joann Skrypzak (English)
Translations: Rene Lauritzen, Sibylle Luig

Graphic design: Ole Mejlby / AGITPROP
Typeface: HEART by Kontrapunkt 2007 / © HEART Herning Museum of Contemporary Art
and Akkurat by Laurenz Brunner
Production: Ines Sutter, Christine Emter (Hatje Cantz)
Reproductions: Cantz Medienmanagement, Hamburg office

Paper: LuxoSamt Offset, 170 g/m^2
Binding: m. appl GmbH & Co. KG, Wemding
Printing: sellier druck GmbH, Freising

Published by
Hatje Cantz Verlag
Zeppelinstrasse 32
73760 Ostfildern
Germany
Tel. +49 711 4405-200
Fax +49 711 4405-220
www.hatjecantz.com

Hatje Cantz books are available internationally at selected bookstores.
For more information about our distribution partners, please visit our homepage at www.hatjecantz.com.

ISBN 978-3-7757-2493-7

Printed in Germany

Cover illustration, front: HEART / View from the north
Cover illustration, back: HEART / Detail of façade
Frontispiece: HEART / View from the northwest

Photo credits:
Roland Halbe Architekturfotografie: cover, frontispiece, 24–53
HEART: 8, 14, 54, 66
Steven Holl Architects: 13, 16, 17, 19, 21, 67, 73, 93
Andy Ryan: 57
Paul Warchol Studio: 59, 61, 63